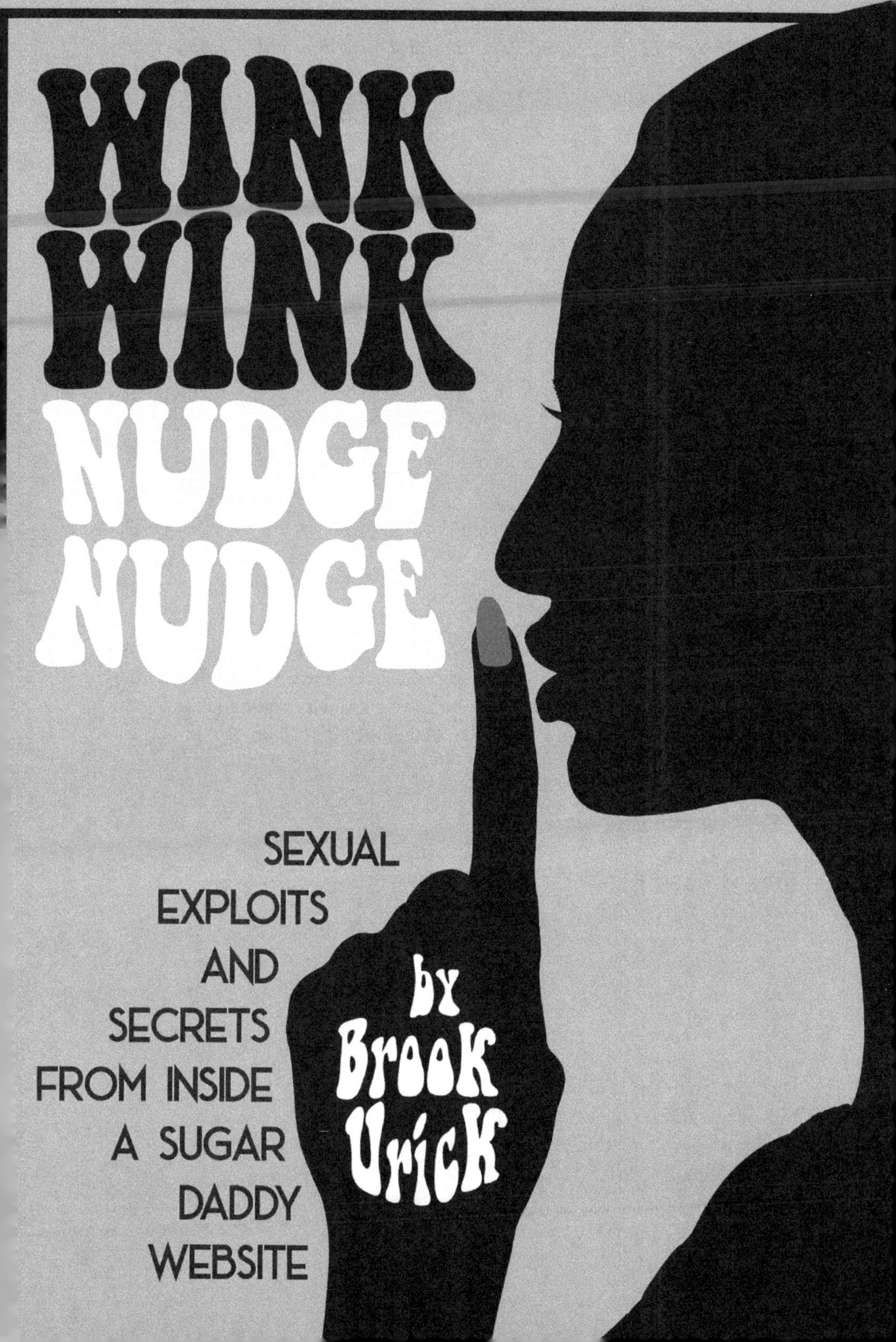
WINK WINK
NUDGE NUDGE
SEXUAL EXPLOITS AND SECRETS FROM INSIDE A SUGAR DADDY WEBSITE
by Brook Urick

WINK WINK NUDGE NUDGE: SEXUAL EXPLOITS AND SECRETS FROM INSIDE A SUGAR DADDY
WEBSITE

Published by:
Trine Day LLC
PO Box 577
Walterville, OR 97489
1-800-556-2012
www.TrineDay.com
trineday@icloud.com

Library of Congress Control Number: 2024944721

Urick, Brook.
WINK WINK NUDGE NUDGE:—1st ed.
p. cm.

Cloth: (ISBN-13) 978-1-63424-470-1
Epub (ISBN-13) 978-1-63424-472-5
TradePaper (ISBN-13) 978-1-63424-471-8
1. SOCIAL SCIENCE/Sex Work & Sex Trade. 2. Online sexual predators Unit-
ed States 3. Sexual commerce. 4. Prostitution Law and legislation United States
Criminal provisions 5. Young women.. I. Urick, Brook. II. Title

FIRST EDITION
10 9 8 7 6 5 4 3 2 1

Distribution to the Trade by:
Independent Publishers Group (IPG)
814 North Franklin Street
Chicago, Illinois 60610
312.337.0747
www.ipgbook.com

Escalus: *How do you live, Pompey? By being a bawd? What do you think of the trade, Pompey? Is it a lawful trade?*

Pompey: *If the law would allow it, sir.*

Escalus: *But the law will not allow it, Pompey; nor it shall not be allowed in Vienna.*

Pompey: *Does Your Worship mean to geld and splay all the youth of the city?*

Escalus: *No, Pompey.*

Pompey: *Truly, sir, in my poor opinion they will to't then. If Your Worship will take order for the drabs and the knaves, you need not fear the bawds.*

–William Shakespeare, *Measure For Measure*

Special thanks to the handful of people who believed in and encouraged me to express my truth despite the potential risks. My publisher, my editor, and my close friends, Camille, Rachel, and Brittany, who gassed me up when I needed it the most. Alexis, who was ride or die partner through it all. Allison, for your courage. My mother for instilling in me a sense of independence and determinism and for designing the cover.

Thanks to the journalists and producers who never ran the story. You showed me the paramount importance of my voice when you chose to withhold this information from the public, allowing the injustices to continue despite having the power to change them. This book is for those who've felt shame, indignity, and embarrassment because of what they encountered after joining a "sugar daddy website." For anyone who was preyed upon – conned, defrauded, abused, victimized, or worse – as a result of Seeking.

Contents

INTRODUCTION

Reflecting on my life's lessons, I began to understand the ways I was lied to and manipulated during my early years. I wrote this book to show you and the world what I went through, how I came to those realizations, my journey. I want you, dear reader, to mold your own conclusions. If you've participated in the lifestyle or hope to escape, these pages will show you that you're not alone. If you're the parent or relative of someone who's been affected by sex work, your understanding and kindness is appreciated. And if you're a journalist, I hope you find the courage to tell the stories that matter. Regardless of who you are, I want my story to encourage you to share yours.

Names and identifying details have been changed, except for a few who gave me permission. Everything I have written here is exactly as I remember it with some conversations edited for clarity. The truth is bad enough, so I don't need to make anything up. Am I a disgruntled employee? Certainly. If you aren't a predator or a sociopath, I think you'll be disgruntled as well after reading my story. But my emotions are more complex than a bunch of sour grapes. I'm disgusted, fed up, and aggravated at the egregious behavior we collectively, *as a society, allow.* We victimize the real victims. We wink and nod at the predators. My general sentiment can be distilled into two short words: *Fuck that.* I won't be silenced. I hope you enjoy and learn from my story. I will endure the consequences of telling the truth.

MAY 2014

She told me because she trusts me, but I wish I didn't know. A secret like this would become a story. I thank her and leave her office when neither of us have spoken for a full minute, a mind-numbing sixty seconds. She thanks me in return, but I'm not sure what either of us is thankful for. Jackie and I communicate with our well-honed telepathy. We caution each other to keep an eye on this potential narrative as our popularity grows. We don't want this to pop up during one of my interviews, those pesky reporters like to dig.

It's no secret that The CEO likes younger women. I toss the so-called facts around, bouncing my sensibilities like a pinball. While I check items off my task list, I try to manage the knot in my gut. I'm confused. Befuddled. I wonder what else he has gotten away with. I wonder how young she was, how young she could have been. Chucking my curiosity, my fingers find my keyboard and fall back into typing mode. I reply to an email from a journalist for *GQ*; she's waiting on a sugar baby case study for her piece.

I'll be busy when I get to D.C. next week. A conference, my first live talk show, flaunting and peddling this fringe sugar daddy website. I tell myself sugaring is a choice, no one is forced to do anything. I don't recall what I told myself when I lost my virginity on a motel room floor when I was thirteen years old. Words like denial and naiveté come to mind. But I'm busy. I remind my inner child to keep her eyes on what is going on right here, right now. My plum job. But I can't stop going over my own recent sugar baby antics: I was desperate for money. The three-hundred-pound guy. The bottle of pinot noir reinforcing my determination for the prize, the promise land for sugar babies. He promised two grand but could only cough up two hundred. I was, in my mind at that moment, a cheap whore.

A bad taste settles in my mouth. This website, SeekingArrangement, takes on a fresh clarity for me. I might as well consider myself a sex worker, and a shitty one at that. Squeezing back the waterworks, I sink into my chair. Jackie approaches and tells me through slivered and permanently grim lips that there's a sugar baby who needs to be talked off a ledge. It's always drama with these girls. I feel for them, caught up in the sugar vortex. It's like that carnival ride where you edge into a large cylinder, lean against the wall, and it starts to spin. When it's finally whizzing fast enough, the floor drops away. But you don't fall, you're pinned to the wall by some mysterious energy that forces you into submission.

* * *

Ping. It's an AOL Instant Messenger request from a screenname I don't know. I scratch my head, pushing back my black and red bangs, still an awkward length from when I cut my hair with a razorblade, post dye job. Maybe it's Ivan? We broke up a few months ago; he was my first boyfriend. I wasn't a virgin, but he was. Having sex was his idea, then after an abstinence-only seminar at school he said we shouldn't have.

The person messages me again and I toggle back to the chat. I'm downloading emo music on Limewire in another window. He says his name is

Jack and that my friend Cece gave him my screenname. Cece had a pic-
nic at Balboa Park for her sixteenth birthday a couple weeks ago in the
grass outside the botanical garden. I first met her in Ocean Beach last year,
we shared a forty-ounce beer on the sand. Cece goes to Narcotics Anonymous after a court mandated sentencing. A few of the NA guys, older
guys, were at her party. I guess I caught someone's eye. Romantic.

Jack sends me messages telling me I'm beautiful, that I'm perfect.
I remember him. He seemed shy, looking at me from underneath a flat
mohawk, thick black ink on his arms and hands. We didn't talk then, but
talking with him now makes my heart race like catching a wave at surf
camp or riding my bike down the big hill out front. Jack is twenty-six. I'm
only fourteen but he says he doesn't mind. He says he wants to be with
me, and I'm in shock. I never thought an older guy would like me enough
to get my screenname from my friend and come on to me. He must think
I'm really pretty, even with my new hair that I know looks weird. My dad
made me take family photos at church and it looked like I was wearing a
helmet.

He sends me messages about wanting to *ravage* me and my belly starts
to tingle. I like it. Jack is in grad school and has a girlfriend, but he doesn't
love her. He's a writer, and he says he wants to write a story about me. He
wishes he could be with someone like me, but he's nervous because I'm so
young. I wonder why he's so scared of me being young. He says I'll understand when I'm older. Why does everyone say that? Why can't he just tell
me? No one has ever talked to me like Jack does. He thinks I'm sexy. I reread his messages and feel the tingle again. I hear a thud; my little brother
playing with foam nun chucks outside my door. I close the chat window
and think about what it would be like to be with Jack. I *have to* meet him.

My mom drops me off at a coffee shop with my book for summer
school, *A Separate Peace* by John Knowles. I'm going for "literate and styl-
ish," like the Taking Back Sunday song. I pretend to read, but I can't focus,
and the page in my palm gets wrinkly and moist. The growl of a turbo motor and there he is, pulling up in a beige Monte Carlo with rust spots on
the bumper. I see his black stubble through the window as he kills the engine. Jack sits with me at a small round table under an oak tree but won't
look me in the eye. I don't get up. Play it cool.

He wants to leave he says, staring down at his worn Doc Martin boots.
He covers his mouth with his hand, nails speckled with chipped black
polish. I toss my paper coffee cup in the trash and follow him to the Monte
Carlo, yanking the heavy passenger door open. The bench seat is warm. I

pull my green and white dress down so my skin isn't touching the stuffing coming through the torn leather. I like being in an older guy's car, but it feels like he doesn't want me here.

Jack doesn't say anything, and I can't think of anything to say either. I stare out the window down a road I'm familiar with, but somehow it seems different. We roll into the parking lot of the Eazy-8 Motel – or the Sleazy-8 as my friends call it – and he parks near an overgrown palm tree at the edge of the crumbling asphalt. I wouldn't say my memories here are great, mostly partying and smoking weed. I lost my virginity in one of those rooms last year.

He says wait here. He jingles keys out of the ignition. I feel hot sun on my face through the window, but now that I'm alone, I don't feel happy anymore. It doesn't feel like he *likes me* likes me, the way he made it seem in the chat. A couple minutes pass and he's back complaining about how expensive the motel is, sixty-five dollars. Jack's eyes dart around the parking lot, scanning our surroundings like the soldier guys in *Black Hawk Down*. He tells me to wait in the car and then come up to the room after a few minutes. I wait like he said, but I'm confused. Is he embarrassed to be seen with me?

The room smells like cigarettes. A dim lamp glows in the corner. Jack shuts the drapes and takes off his shirt. A dragon tattoo covers his back, and a black spider web across his stomach. I offer him a condom. I'm not sure how it works. He doesn't take it. He lights a cigarette and sits on the corner of the bed, rubbing the spot next to him with his hand. I crawl over across a gold duvet that feels like it's made of plastic.

He puts out his cigarette with one hand and hikes up my dress with the other. He removes my panties and puts his mouth between my legs, his lips big and wet. I'm not sure what he's doing. I see his reflection in the mirror on the dresser, a mess of black and green ink. After a minute, he stands up and unbuckles his belt, pulling his pants down to his ankles. Before I know it, he mounts me and grinds his hips into mine. I don't feel anything, is this right? He moans and seconds later it's over. He says he's sorry, but sorry for what? He moves to the sink, and while bent over, his dark mohawk hangs in his eyes like a horse's mane. He mutters something, splashing water on his face. *Get dressed*, he says again, louder.

I find my panties and push my legs through the lace. My heart pounds. Why are we leaving so soon? He said he wanted me, but now he just wants me to leave. Did I do something wrong? I follow him to the car. I'm dizzy and inside me feels like quicksand. I could throw up, but I don't want to upset him even more. He makes me promise not to tell anyone, his knuckles gripping the metal steering wheel. My mom tells me I'm good at keeping secrets. I won't tell anyone.

PART ONE
2013

Age: 21
Playlist: Disclosure, Daft Punk, Drake
TV: *The Vampire Diaries, Scandal, South Park*
Favorite pastime: Raving, cooking, smoking weed

CHAPTER 1

THE SEX INDUSTRY

Blood starts to pool in my cuticle, tracing the curve around my sparkly blue acrylic nail. The warehouse smells like Lean Cuisines and pumpkin spice candles as I pat the drop with a tissue. The cardboard leaves awful cuts if I'm not careful. The boxes are for our products, a sex toy.

I work for an adult novelty wholesaler, a manufacturer of a male chastity device. It's exactly as weird as it sounds, especially for a nineteen-year-old. It's odd that I'm technically working in the sex industry, but sure beats working at Zumiez. If I ever have to grip another skateboard deck, I'll scream.

This is basically just a warehouse where we ship out plastic cock cages. I do some bookkeeping in QuickBooks, put the product in boxes, and man the phones, by far the worst part. It's always some cuck with his dick in his hand. I get they don't have anyone to talk to about this, and I'm sort of an expert. So, I take the phone calls. But *Jesus fucking Christ*, these guys are a bunch of weirdos.

"Hello, how can I help you?"

"Hi, um, I just have a question," a small voice says on the other end of the line.

It's a niche product, a medical grade polycarbonate cock cage designed for long term wear. A plastic cage goes over the shaft and a ring behind the testicles, trapping them between the cage and ring so it can't be removed. There's a pin that goes through the top with a small padlock. Men who wear it are interested in the fetish of orgasm denial, or just looking to try something new. Like I said, a bunch of weirdos. After working here for two years, I'm numb to them at this point.

"Sure, what's your question," I recognize this guy's voice. He's called before. He probably just wants to hear me answer the questions again.

"Well, um, I'm just wondering if you're thinking about making a micro version. I'm too small for the cages," he explains. "I'm only about an inch flaccid."

This guy has a certified micro penis. The men with tiny dicks always want people to know. "It's a great idea, and I'll pass it on to the designers." I lie.

"Okay, um, do you know of any companies that make a smaller cage?"

I'm allowed to tell these guys to fuck off, but I refrain because I know he'd probably like it. "I don't, I'm sorry." I decide to be short with him because I need to finish this shipment so I can get home.

"Um, okay, can I ask you another question?"

"Sure," I reply, wrapping a Band-Aid around my finger.

"Um, do you keep your boyfriend in one?"

Oh yeah, I keep a whole fleet of men locked up. They sleep in kennels and worship my feet. "I'm a lesbian," I tell him in my most butch voice.

"Oh, um, okay. Thanks."

"No problem, you have a nice day." *Click.*

Chapter 2

Aaron

My boyfriend, Aaron, makes fake IDs. That's how we met. Being under twenty-one in a city like Las Vegas is torture, so having a fake is a rite of passage. Thankfully I only have six months left before my twenty-first birthday.

He met me at my office one afternoon to take my photo for the ID. Aaron tossed a light blue sheet over the back of a door, and I couldn't help but notice the perfect pecs peeking out from under his purple deep V-neck. We instantly clicked. Now nearly a year later, we're still dating and talking about moving in together.

I'm at work perusing Facebook and find a notification in a folder called "other messages." It's from someone I don't know, but they seem to know me.

"I know you don't believe us, but Aaron is a bad person. He's been cheating on you for eight months..."

My heart sinks. I am completely blindsided by these five paragraphs describing in startling detail the intricacies of my and Aaron's relationship and the relationship he was carrying on simultaneously with another girl. Like his mattress that disappeared, the first place we ever had sex. He told me he gave it to a fraternity brother. The letter says he gave it to this other girlfriend, which is why it was mysteriously missing. The examples go on. It's been over between them for months, and I'm the last one to find out.

My sinuses swell and the tears and heaving hit me like a wave. Of course, there were signs. Ignoring my texts at night, girl's clothes in his laundry, a love note in his car. Then there were the yeast infections. I was blinded by love, but there was no hiding behind convenient excuses anymore. Aaron and I are so over.

I take a deep inhale; the tears keep streaming. With a jaw clenched, my taste for petty vengeance takes over. I print out the Facebook essay and write my own message to Aaron in Sharpie over it:

Fuck you, don't ever contact me again. I knew it, and you covered it up so well. You're a pathological liar and I'm lucky this kind woman told me the truth. Bye forever, douchebag.

I can hardly see the road, crying so hard snot is running down my face. I drive to my house to collect Aaron's belongings. I leave his shit on his doorstep with the note. A few hours later, my phone rings and Aaron's caller ID photo appears, a picture of his torso. I seethe.

"This is the last time you'll ever talk to me, Aaron, so say whatever you need to because there is absolutely no chance."

"I just want you to know how sorry I am. I never loved her the way I love you," he says. "I made a mistake."

A big mistake. *Huge.* I crawl into my bed in nothing but my underwear, too broken to find sweats or a hoodie. Through my pounding headache and random dry heaves, I can barely hear my own thoughts. How could he? If someone who said he loved me can do this, I'm not sure love is what I want.

CHAPTER 3

THE "BALLER"

"Brook, Come to STK with me! Some guys from the bar invited us," Jasmin shouts down the hall. "I want a filet mignon," she says.

She's rummaging through the closet in our third bedroom looking for her other shoe. I don't know how she managed to lose just one. It's the two of us living here, a pair of college girls with sinking couch cushions and a sink full of dirty dishes. I just turned twenty-one and we party every weekend. I'm inches from the bathroom mirror, picking at a zit on my chin when she poses the question. I load the bong and take a long drag, my exhale filling the hall with haze. I lean against the door frame.

"But it's raining, and I was going to make salmon," I say, and let out a booming cough. A soft drizzle falls outside the window.

"We're in no position to turn down a free meal, bitch. Plus, there will be rich guys there." Jasmin punches a silver heel into the air. "I found it!" she squeals.

The details pique my interest. After several bong loads and even more coats of mascara, we arrive at the Cosmopolitan fashionably late. We meet three dapper looking older men at a booth. They're from Newport they say. The alpha introduces himself as Kris, waving hello with a glitzy watch on his wrist. It looks heavy. His stocky build and beady blue eyes remind me of Sean Austin, the actor who plays a hobbit in Lord of the Rings.

"We ordered one of everything," he says.

I figure he's being glib, but the table fills with literally one of each appetizer. We feast. Kris is coming off a big win and he's in chipper spirits. He wants to hit the blackjack table after dinner and slips Jasmin and me a few crisp hundreds to wager. At twenty-five bucks a hand, the money goes fast. I'm not lucky, so I decide to go home. Jasmin stays.

The next morning, she calls. "What are you doing? Come to Fashion Show," she says. "Kris is wondering about you. We're shopping."

Could this guy be into me? Perhaps a sugar daddy scenario? I must find out. I throw on a chambray button down and meet them in the bathing suit section of Nordstrom. Kris is talking on the phone while perusing trunks. Jasmin is wearing the same clothes as the night before.

"Hey bitch, you made it. Look at this this cover up." She holds up the garment.

"That's cute," I skim one of the racks. "How much stuff are you getting?" I'm hesitant to go overboard. What if he really likes me? Maybe I should play the long game.

"I'm definitely getting these," she says with a handful of swim attire. "I want some wedges." She trails off, her voice fades.

Do I only get a bathing suit and act overly grateful while she goes ham? I decide on two suits and a crop top. This is enough that I don't squander the opportunity, but not so much that I overindulge and send the wrong message. Jasmin gets the same, plus a couple cover ups and the wedges. She peers at my haul on the sales counter.

"That's all you're getting?"

"Yeah, this is good. What are you doing after this?" I want to see how far I can ride this gravy train.

"We're going to Anaheim," Kris chimes in as he comes up behind us with pants and a sneaker box. "You should come. We'll be back tomorrow."

He sets the items down and pulls a wad of cash from his pocket. The total is over twelve hundred. I don't work until Monday and a rendezvous with a daddy-type sounds exactly like what I need post-breakup. I've barely eaten anything for weeks so I'm super skinny right now. The suits will look great.

"You swear we'll be back tomorrow?" I say, pretending to waffle.

"I swear," Kris assures me.

He's about five eight and tubbier than I remember. I'm not sure if he and Jasmin hooked up last night. She didn't come home. She and I head home to pack a few essentials and agree to meet Kris at the airport a couple hours later. It's 3PM and Kris is hammered, drunk. He's near the luggage drop with his suitcase flung open on the floor. Hundred-dollar bills are strewn amongst his clothes as he frantically searches for something.

"I can't find my ID," he mutters and raises his head. His face is flushed, and his drunk eyes gaze at us, but past us. I give Jasmin the look.

"I'll help you," she kneels and begins searching. After a few minutes, she uncovers his passport. The ID is still MIA, but this will suffice. We approach the counter and I realize we're buying one-way tickets in cash onsite. *So sketch.* Kris struggles with his words, his ability to speak, with the Southwest employee.

"You can't have more than ten thousand in cash per person," she mentions after seeing the money in his suitcase.

"Can you take some of this?" Kris motions to the mess of bills among his clothing and other paraphernalia.

We don't want to risk getting stopped by security, so Jasmin and I each put a couple thousand in our purses. The agent accepts the money for our tickets and prints our boarding passes for the next flight to LAX. We make the flight, winnings in tow. Once we land, I realize Kris hasn't planned for the forty-mile ride to Anaheim. Luckily, I recently downloaded a new app for a black car service called Uber. Within fifteen minutes, I have a Town Car pulling up for us.

"Let me know how much I owe you," Kris smiles, impressed with my little trick.

We head out to meet his friends for a chartered party bus to a nightclub. Our Uber pulls up to a modest green home with a grass lawn. The total is a hundred and seventy-five with tip.

Kris gives me two crumpled hundreds. "Keep the change."

I shove them into my Coach wristlet and pull the skirt of my blue halter dress down; it barely covers my butt. The plan: HEAT Ultra Lounge for his friend's rap gig. Inside the club, Kris apparently takes a liking to our server and requests $500 in ones from her. He wants to make it rain. Following the friend's set, he does just that. Party people go berserk as money spins in the air like a cash cyclone. I debate grabbing for it but don't want to seem desperate, so I casually pocket seven dollars. After the club, we taxi to a nearby hotel and book a double queen. I sleep in one bed while Kris and Jasmin share the other. I'm glad I don't have to sleep next to Kris, especially when I wake up to him snoring with his arm around Jasmin. Brunch is awkward with the three of us. He tells us about his mom who passed a year ago, a full-on moment. His main business, he tells us, is sports betting.

"Do you ever want to help me with bets while I'm in Newport? I can give you a kickback if we win."

"Sure," I say.

Moonlighting as a bookie would be a welcome second income stream. I make it back to Vegas unscathed with two new bathing suits. Not bad. Two nights later, Kris calls to invite Jasmin and me back to the Cosmo where he and his friend Roman are staying. We meet them on the fourteenth floor in a wrap-around suite.

"Dude, we were on the roof of Marquee last night." Roman says. "You can get up there from the balcony." Jasmin and I go out there to check. Outside we see how easy it would be to climb from the rail to the roof of the adjacent building. Roman kneels to give us a boost. "C'mon, I'll help."

"Do not go up there!" Kris barks from the kitchen. "They already yelled at us!" His warning falls on deaf ears, and after a few drinks Roman helps us up.

The bass booms at Marquee, and lights sparkle at the edge of the roof. Jasmin and I snap a picture for Instagram before Kris screams at us to get down. We hustle off and apologize. Ten minutes later security is at the door with a raucous knock. We really weren't supposed to go out there. Three men in suits politely tell us we need to leave … Kris and Roman included. They are being evicted.

"Roman! What the actual fuck." Kris is fuming, and they pack up their things under the supervision of security.

Downstairs in the lobby, we stand next to their bags while Kris is on the phone frantically trying to arrange another comped room. Jasmin and I decide to bow out, apologizing profusely.

A couple weeks later, Kris calls for a favor. He's back in Newport and wants me to place a sports bet for him like we talked about. The catch, I need to act now, one of the games is about to start. I look at the digital clock on my nightstand and notice a wine ring stain on the varnish.

"Uhm, I don't have the money for that," I say, still feeling a little guilty for getting him kicked out of the Cosmo.

"Just go to the nearest casino and I'll pay you back. This is a sure thing, so you can take it out of the profit," he says. "I'll share some with you, too."

I'm conflicted. Do I use my own money and risk losing? It seems suspect, but he is so certain about the win and about paying me back. *What do I have to lose?* Well, exactly $500.

"You better not be using your own money," Jasmin warns after overhearing our phone call.

"Oh, I'm not," I lie.

I know Kris has plenty of funds. This bet was pennies compared to the Benjamins he flaunted on our little adventure, a drop in the bucket to him. There's barely enough in my checking account to cover it. With a deep breath, I ante up. No risk, no reward, right? I grip the steering wheel and drive to South Point, all the while thinking this is a stupid fucking idea.

But he's rich, and this could end up being a lucrative side hustle, a gamble in more ways than one. I pull the money from my sad checking account at the ATM and traipse toward the sports book, staring at the cash in hand before placing my bet.

I read off the text Kris sent me, money line run line something. It's gibberish to me. I take a picture of the ticket and send it to Kris who says he's grateful. He asks for my banking details and guarantees he'll send the reimbursement. Within a few hours, the games are over, and the ticket is a loser. Kris goes dark. I call him. No response. I call from my work phone the next day and get through. He insists that his friend already sent the money. He directs me to a Western Union. I go, but there is no transfer for me.

Days go by and still nothing. I text Kris, asking him what his mom would think of him scamming a broke college student. He blocks me. I guess I took it too far. I can't believe I fell for a man's bullshit, once again. With my tail between my legs and my bank account drained, I sulk in shame and do not tell Jasmin. I'll get rent money some other way. Maybe I'll call my dad. My mom used to tell me he's self-centered, but I rarely see him since I moved to Las Vegas five years ago. It might be time to cash in on his absent-father guilt.

CHAPTER 4

IT'S FREE TO JOIN

My friend Christine's apartment is on the fourth floor in a trendy complex in South Las Vegas. It's a modern building with three pools and underground parking. She comes down to get me wearing a tight bodycon dress that barely covers her crotch, paired with pink Uggs. She's a model, so she looks good in everything.

"Hi babe! You look amazing, love the shoes!" I say from across the parking lot.

We're having a night out at a new club called The Light at Mandalay Bay. She knows one of the hosts. He usually puts us at tables with rich guys because we're sort of a commodity that way. We get to party with free champagne, and the men get to feel important and desired. The ballers only want to ball out if they can do it in front of hot girls. I don't even like drinking, but I love the way I feel with a glass of Dom Perignon in my hand that I didn't pay for. It tastes like bath water, but the bottle glows in the dark. I'd much rather wade through potential suitors at the club than fish for a date on Tinder. The app is addicting, but the matches are usually duds. Like the guy who brought Christine and me to a hotel suite where we were promptly kicked out by his mom. So embarrassing.

We take the elevator up to Christine's place. It smells like fresh linen. Glade plugins pepper the walls. Her unit has high ceilings, long navy-blue drapes, and a small balcony overlooking the parking lot. Another friend, Shayla, gets up from the couch to greet me.

"Hi Brookie!" she squeals. Shayla is voluptuous and an Instagram star. She knows how to twerk and tried to teach me once, but I still don't know how.

"What are you guys doing?" I ask, noticing a new MacBook on the ottoman. There's an orange and red webpage on the display. It looks like a website some grandpa would use.

"Just searching for daddies on SA," Shayla says with a sarcastic laugh.

She obviously means sugar daddies. Christine has told me about the website before, SeekingArrangement, SA for short. My only real experience with these sorts of characters was with Kris, a lying scammer. That can't be the type she's talking about.

"What, you mean like rich guys? Isn't that what we're going to the club for?"

"Well yeah, but these guys give you money," Christine says as though she has been the recipient of some of this money.

I've only ever been swindled out of it, so the concept is new to me. But I'm on Tinder and fairly used to dating online. I get the appeal with its convenience and wide range of possibilities. SA touts itself as a website for "mutually beneficial arrangements," whatever that means.

"So, you meet people on there who just give you money?" I'm skeptical.

"Kinda, I mean my main sugar daddy is actually Shayla's cousin." Christine smiles with an air of self-satisfaction. "You remember him."

I do. We met briefly at Christine's house a few months ago. I did not get the vibe that he was a sugar daddy.

"Huh, okay. How do you know they're rich?"

"You just see what they're like. Some guys are fake, but so are a lot of the guys at the club." Shalya shrugs, picks up a file and chisels her long pink nails. They have rhinestones and bows and match her iPhone case.

"It's free. You should sign up," Christine says. "They're casting for a reality show. We could be the next Kim K!"

Now she's speaking my language. I know everyone thinks this, but someone should make a reality show about us. We live a glamorous life, despite being college students with no money to speak of. Seems like the perfect premise. Plus, I'm a tad envious of Shayla's Instagram fame and could use some clout like that of my own.

"A reality show? Okay, maybe." Not gonna lie ... the prospect of quitting my eighteen dollar an hour job for the life of a reality star strikes a chord. I bet the guys who ignored me in high school would lose their shit if they saw me on TV.

Back home the next day, I log onto SeekingArrangement and create my profile. The site feels straight out of 2005. No wonder old dudes are on here; it's archaic. I can't find anything about the show casting, so I text Christine. She forwards me the email. It's from casting@seekingarrangement.com, and the signature says his name is Anthony. Seems legit.

> HEY ANTHONY,
> One of my friends told me to join this site and apply for your casting call, and I'm so excited! I just got verified. My profile number is 1676570.

My phone number is 619XXXXXXX and you can use this email to contact me anytime if you think I'd be right for the show. My number is from San Diego because that's where I'm from, but I live here in Vegas.

Just a thought, two of my friends use the site too (Christine and Shayla) and it might be an interesting dynamic to have girls that are actually friends on the show for the chemistry. Also, we're hilarious and gorgeous.

I find some of my best pictures from Instagram. Me in the pool at Marquee Day Club, posing in a cowgirl outfit and sipping a cocktail at who knows which club. Within twenty minutes of hitting send, my phone rings.

"This is Anthony with SeekingArrangement casting. How are you?" The voice on the other end has a sing-song quality like a used car salesman.

"Hey, I'm good, thanks for calling." I try to contain my excitement.

"You're perfect for this opportunity," Anthony says. "We just need you to come for an on camera interview this Saturday. The compensation is $250."

"That sounds great. But I just signed up, so I've never really used the site. Is that okay?"

"Totally fine. I'll walk you through what to say. We just need you to show up looking good and ready to have a good time," Anthony says.

Two hundred and fifty dollars? Just to show up? That seems like a deal I can't refuse. This is my chance to get discovered! I can't pass it up.

"Okay thanks! Oh, and my friends also applied for the casting, Christine and Shayla. Can they come too?"

"Did they? I didn't get their email. Tell them to resend it and I'll give them a call. I'll email you the details."

"Okay, awesome! See you then!" I am ecstatic. I've never been on TV before, but once they meet me, they're going to offer me my own show for sure. I can feel it. I text Christine and Shayla to tell them about the call from Anthony. We're going to be the next Kardashians!

Chapter 5

Casting Director/ Public Relations Manager

*P*ing. It's an email from Anthony asking me to sign the media agreement for the filming tomorrow. I've never had to sign anything like this before, so I better actually read it.

> I _____, (legal name) understand that in exchange for compensation from "SeekingArrangement. com," I agree to share my experiences to the media of its choosing. I also agree to release "SeekingArrangement.com" of any blame in my experience and will not speak negatively on its behalf.

I'm not sure what experiences he's talking about since I've never had any, but sure. It seems strange that I would need to sign a contract saying I won't speak negatively about the site. Does that happen? Whatever, I'll agree to that.

> _____ (initial) I am in accordance with SeekingArrangement. com's terms of use and have never accepted money for sex or solicited sex for money.

That's also a little weird. Why would they think I've accepted money for sex? Again, I'm not going to argue.

> _____ (initial) I agree to keep the terms of my agreement with Infostream Group Inc. confidential, or this contract will be void, unless otherwise stated or authorized by an executive party.

So I can't mention there's a contract, got it. Initial.

> _____ (initial) I understand that this agreement is legal and binding. And by signing this document I hereby promise to participate and appear on the show.

This seems odd ... "hereby promise." That doesn't sound very legal to me, but whatever.

InfoStream Group Inc. agrees to pay participant $350 in exchange for media appearance or participation. InfoStream Group Inc. retains the right to forego compensation if the participant does not abide by the aforementioned terms.

I thought it was two-fifty? Anthony must not be very meticulous with these "agreements." I'm at work, so I print the contract and sign on the dotted lines. Then I snap a picture and send it back to Anthony. He responds a few minutes later.

> Hi Brook,
>
> Perfect, thanks! Please arrive at the Palms Hotel at 11:40 AM tomorrow, as it may take 5-10 minutes to locate the actual lounge.
>
> Finally, please do not mention that you are getting compensated. Sometimes, the outlet will take offense and assume that we are paying models/actors who are not members of the site. FYI, we are just showing our gratitude for your participation.
>
> If you have any questions, please let me know. Looking forward to tomorrow!
>
> Best,
> Anthony Varaz
> Manager, Public Relations
> SeekingArrangement.com
> (702) 635-XXXX
> Press@SeekingArrangemetn.com

Oh my god ... the Travel Channel! I wonder what kind of reality show this is. I'm not going to ask too many questions, but I'm super excited to find out. It's weird that he doesn't want me to say I got paid. Is it not obvious? Why would I show up if I wasn't being paid? Anthony's signature says he's the Public Relations Manager. I thought he was the Casting Director? He must be important. But his email address is misspelled, so maybe not that important.

The big day. I park in the structure at the Palms and get a text from Anthony. It says he's at the shark. The shark? That must be a typo. I get out of the car, and I'm hit with the hellish heat that bakes this city in the summer. I fluff the ruffles on my cream-colored camisole and fix my black pencil skirt that's stuck to my thighs with sweat. I brush a curl away from my face and reapply my nude lipstick. *Reality show, here I come.*

My black pumps click on the tile as I walk through the casino looking for the sea creature. Then I see it. There is a giant shark suspended in what looks like blue liquid as a focal point for this bar.

"Anthony?" I ask the only guy sitting there.

Anthony turns and smiles. He has little gaps between his front teeth. "Brook!" He gets up, and I'm shocked at how short he is. I'm towering over him. He's wearing a cheap blue suit and drinking an Old Fashioned. "Do you want a drink?" he asks.

I order a vodka soda with a splash of cranberry because I think that's what mature women drink. The bartender cards me, so I must not look that mature. I'm only twenty-one, so I want to seem as composed as possible if I'm going to land a role as a reality star. Or maybe I should act crazy? The crew is setting up the shot nearby in the corner of the bar, slot machines in the background. I sip my drink.

There is a pervasive odor in this bar, sort of a mix between mildew, stale drinks, and American Spirits. When my parents got divorced and I was forced to spend every other weekend with my father and his new wife, I became super sensitive to strange smells. Their house smelled like it was haunted by the ghosts of cigarettes past.

"This is going to be really simple." Anthony is oblivious to my concerns, my trepidation. "They'll interview you and a sugar daddy, then we might go up to the club for another shot. He's late, but he'll be here soon." He looks down at his phone.

"What is this show about?" I ask, trying not to seem eager.

"Well, it's for the Travel Channel, and it's about the wildest parts of Las Vegas. A one-off," he says, typing into his Blackberry.

A fucking one-off? I don't know much about reality shows but a one-off does not scream "big break" to me. I adjust my posture and recalibrate my expectations. At least I'll get to meet a real sugar daddy. Maybe he'll ask me out.

Megan from the production team finds us at the bar. She's thin, wearing all black. "Is this our girl?" She asks and flashes a half-hearted smile at me.

"Yeah, it is. Brook, meet Megan."

She smiles and nods. "Is the sugar daddy here yet?"

Anthony looks at his phone again. "He should be here soon."

"Okay, we're ready whenever he gets here," Megan says. She taps her watch. It's 12:30PM. At this point, he's about an hour late.

"Let me give him a call," Anthony says and hops off the barstool. A few minutes later, he saunters back to the bar, defeated. "He can't make it,

had something else come up. But don't worry, I'm going to do it instead."
Yikes, poor Anthony. He walks off to inform Megan about the change of
plans, then waves me over to the set up.

"Alright, let's get started," Megan says. "Brook, I'll have you sit here."
She motions to a low black armchair. "And Anthony, you on the left."

Anthony on the left? Now I'm confused. I thought they were going to
be interviewing me, but it looks like they're interviewing both of us. Together? Is he supposed to be … my sugar daddy? I take a seat under a
rack of blinding lights and squint. I can hardly make out Megan and some
colleague of hers behind the cameras.

"Can you hold hands?" she asks and glances up from her monitor.

It feels like someone is turning my uterus like a doorknob. My breath
is shallow and my skin prickles. I survey the angles, wondering if they can
tell how much taller I am in the shot. I'm going to look huge on camera!
This is not how I wanted my reality show debut to unfold. Anthony offers
his hand and I force myself to take it. Megan starts asking questions, and
I go numb.

"So, what sort of things do you do together?" Megan asks.

I have no idea what to say but manage to come up with, "I love to go
on dates to nice restaurants, out to clubs, and of course, shopping!" I let
out a nervous laugh.

"And Anthony, how much do you make?"

"My income is six figures, upper six figures." he lies.

His cheap blue suit tells another story. Megan asks us a few more questions, but she can tell I'm uncomfortable. I look to Anthony for answers
to most of her inquiries. She wraps it up when she realizes I have nothing
of value to say.

"Okay, thanks. We're going to get some b-roll. You can go back to the
bar." She practically rolls her eyes.

Anthony buys another round of drinks. I want to leave, but I don't want
to screw up my chances if there actually *is* a reality show on the horizon.

"So, what are they doing?" I ask, trying to make conversation.

"B-roll is like when you have shots of people just hanging out, no au-
dio. We pretend to be talking, laughing, having a good time," Anthony
says with a cheesy grin.

I am having anything but a good time. I muster another fake laugh.
Even if I sucked at the interview, I'm going to nail this b-roll. Megan lets
us know that the shoot is over. It's only 1:15PM, but it feels like hours have
passed. Anthony pays the tab, and we get up to leave.

"I have another gig for you if you'd be interested," he says. "We're shooting stock photography next week with The CEO for one of our new dating sites. Compensated, of course. I can email you the details."

"Sure, I can do that. Thanks for the opportunity. This was really cool, too," I say.

I shuffle back to the parking garage in my fast fashion and feel a sense of relief with a sprinkle of kismet. I might not have a reality show deal, but I did learn a couple new skills: fibbing on camera and fake laughing. That Anthony guy sucks. I'm going to take his job.

CHAPTER 6

THE INTRODUCTION

I head up to the tenth floor of the MGM Grand and knock on room 10225. I've never been up here before and it's a legitimate maze, but this room was easy to find. I call Anthony to let him know I'm here. He opens the door, and he's as short as I remember.

"Brook, come in! Do you want a glass of champagne?" he asks, holding up a bottle of Barefoot sparkling wine.

I glance around the one-bedroom suite where there are three models posing on a sectional with an unassuming man whose wearing an MIT shirt. He's sitting on the back of the couch holding a stick attached to dangling carrots on a string. I'm surprised at how campy this is, the actual vegetables he's holding over the models. I guess I was expecting a photoshoot in a studio, or something, instead of a renegade project in a hotel suite. At least they have drinks.

"Sure, I'll have a glass."

Sensing my obvious confusion, Anthony attempts to explain the scene. "This is for a new app called Carrot Dating. The idea is that men can bribe their way into a date by offering gifts."

"Carrots? Not the diamond kind I presume." I try for a joke. Anthony doesn't catch it.

The room is dark. My head hurts. I've already had enough of this bullshit. The photographer is wearing a t-shirt with a suit vest, crouching in front of the sofa looking for an angle. The models each have a different look. One is brunette and sort of average, one is petite with black hair, and the third is platinum blond with a voluptuous frame. All are white, as am I.

"Can you all position your legs the same? And can you look at the carrot like you want to eat it?" The models oblige, biting their lips and widening their eyes. The blond raises a finger to her mouth and points at the carrot with the other hand. "That's it, perfect."

My tummy twists, which could be the glass of bubbly I enjoyed on an empty stomach. Or it could be something else. I wonder if anyone I know will see these pictures. Is this even worth the money? I guess it's too late to wonder now.

I feel Anthony's hand on my back and flinch. I'm reminded of when I had to hold it during that terrible interview and am struck with a case of the heebie-jeebies. He directs me to the bathroom where two hair and makeup artists are waiting for me. My makeup and hair are already done, and they tell me I look great as we all study my reflection. My eyes are bloodshot from the pot or the booze. I'm nervous. The other models are older and more experienced, considering I have absolutely no experience at all.

"Alright, we're ready for you," Anthony waves me into the main room.

The man from the couch is standing on a white background holding those damn carrots. I was hoping I wouldn't have to be opposite a vegetable. "This is Brook, she's one of the last-minute models I called. She did the Travel Channel piece for us," Anthony says. "Brook, this is The CEO."

"Oh, hi," The CEO responds, uninterested, his face five inches from his white iPhone.

He's about six foot tall with plenty of nervous energy. I get the sense he's got somewhere else to be. He rapid-fires text messages while a makeup artist pats the oil and sweat from his forehead.

A plumpish woman with dirty blonde hair parted at the side hangs over in the corner. "I'm Jackie," she says, giving me a close-lipped smile. "I'm the PR manager." I thought Anthony was the PR manager? Whatever, this whole company is a shit-show.

I take a deep breath and force a smile. "I'm Brook."

"We're going to have you kneeling in front of him, looking at the carrot like you want to eat it." Anthony paces back and forth in front of the set.

Seriously? I guess it's better than having to take my clothes off. I feel like an idiot, but I oblige and face the camera. The CEO is behind me holding the carrots over my head. It's all very cringe. When we break, I toss back a second glass of sparkling wine to take the edge off. There's a knock at the door and a skinny young lady in a striped tube top emerges. She looks younger than me, overdone in blue eyeshadow, blonde bob tucked behind her ears. She seems reserved and has the physique of a pre-teen.

"Tanya, you're here!" Anthony greets her.

"That's The CEO's wife," Jackie tells me. "We're getting some shots of the two of them."

After a few pictures of the happy couple, the two head out for dinner leaving us to wrap the shoot. There's an energy shift when they make their exit. Like dad is gone and the kids are in charge.

"This is *not* what our jobs are like every day," Jackie says, swirling a glass of rosé.

She tells me this is her second year working for The CEO. She started when the company was just six people in a condo. Tanya was also one of the original employees. The CEO initially hired her as customer support but decided to wife her up instead. She's twenty-three and they've been married about a year. Jackie looks right at me and asks me if I have a job.

"Right now, I work for an adult novelty company," I say.

Jackie acts surprised. "What's that like?"

"It's a fringe product for fetish customers and adult-toy enthusiasts. I'm not into it personally, but after working there for three years, I'm sort of an expert."

I give her the whole spiel. Wide-eyed, Jackie listens while I drop sex industry buzzwords and elucidate the intricacies of tease play. I never thought this knowledge would come in handy, but my party trick seems to impress her.

"You're really good at talking about sex," she says. "You should work for us."

"I'm still in school, but maybe when I'm done!" I say, flattered.

"Alright, this is the last shot. It's a pillow fight," Anthony says, clutching a pillow in one hand and a pocketknife in the other. "It's okay," he says, holding up the pillow, "I brought this one from home."

He proceeds to stab it open, white feathers poofing out all over the room. The three other models and I pose for a fake pillow fight on the bed, feathers swirling. There's also a male model holding a giant Sugar Daddy candy on a stick, using it as a paddle to spank our butts. Is this for real? Jackie has to leave. She says she's driving to Disneyland with her ten-year-old son. We exchange numbers before she heads out.

A week later, she texts me asking if I want to interview for a PR coordinator position at SA. I still have another year of college, but I enjoy the idea. Before I get any big girl job, I'm going to try my luck as a sugar baby. How hard can it be? I log into my account and come up with this for my profile:

Headline: Hey boys
Occupation: Student
Expectation: Moderate $$
Body Type: Athletic

About Me
I am an extrovert, a confident, real girl who enjoys fine dining

and being treated well. I have a great job, amazing friends and everything I need but am looking to supplement with a fantastic man who can treat me right. I like sparkly things and mid-century modern decor. My above average appearance is paralleled only by my articulate wit. It would be my pleasure to be seen on the arm of a strong, supportive man.

WHAT I'M LOOKING FOR:
Living in Las Vegas, I'm looking for someone who can keep up with my lifestyle and also keep me company. I would like to experience lavish settings, lush vacations and complimentary benefits of a man who knows what kind of treatment a lady like me deserves and isn't afraid to show me.

Off to the races.

Chapter 7

First Date

My SA inbox is filled with sugar daddies. Most of them are asking for sex. Messages like "500 no condom" are the norm. I get it, the site is basically for men who want to sleep with girls out of their league and are willing to pay for it. I'm not going to agree to sex with someone I've never met, but I could really use the money. After getting scammed by Kris, it's been hard to recover. Plus, I'm paying for my own college tuition. Being an adult is expensive.

I'm not having any luck finding men on Tinder. They all want sex too, but they don't have a dollar to spare and want to go Dutch. If I like the guy, and he happens to give me money, what's the difference? It's not like I want to fall in love right now anyway. After Aaron, succumbing to love and the vulnerability that comes with it is out of the question. This way, I'm in control of my emotions.

I set up my first date with a guy named John. Fitting. He doesn't have a picture on his profile but sends me one via text. His face isn't visible, but he seems nice enough and is purportedly in the movie business. I'm to meet him on a Saturday night at the Hard Rock Hotel Circle Bar. I call when I arrive.

"I'm wearing a black hat," he tells me over the phone.

I scan the area and spot him at a table. He's fatter than his picture implied. We sit down at a small table and a cocktail waitress serves me, then overserves me. Within an hour I've thrown back three glasses of Pinot Noir. There are pterodactyls in my gut that stir up a nasty case of hiccups.

"You're so beautiful," he flatters me, adjusting his t-shirt over his belly. "I'm having a hard time hearing you though." John points to his ear and shrugs.

It's not that loud, so I speak louder between hiccups. I feel my face turn red when I can hardly get through a sentence.

"Let's go up to my room so we can talk," he says.

I agree. He looks old for 47. Maybe he's trying to appear younger with his black cadet hat. There's a liter of SKYY vodka in his suite – no ice, no mixer – but I'm already drunk. I ask for water instead. With his back turned, he pours some into a plastic cup at the minibar and brings it to me.

"Where would your dream vacation be?" he asks, sweetly holding my left hand. I pet the blue velvet fabric of the sectional with my right hand.

"Probably Greece or Italy. I've never been to Europe," I say hoping he'll take me.

"You know, I have a trip to Aruba planned and need someone to bring." He squeezes my hand, musters his sincerest gaze, and says, "I want you to come with me and be my sugar baby."

Wow, that was easy. It seems I've found exactly what SA promises. I must be so fortunate to find it on the first date. Lucky me. John is no prize, but he's also not awful. His stubble grazes my cheek, and he reeks of booze. He grabs my breast and lifts my chiffon skirt. I go along with it. I want to be wanted, and this is the price I pay as an object of his desire. I mean, he's taking me on a tropical vacation. It's the least I can do. The next thing I know, he's on top of me on the couch, unbuttoning his pants.

"I want you so bad," he says, panting and licking my neck.

I let him take what he wants, too drunk to care. It lasts all of thirty seconds, and I can barely stand once it's over. I usually don't get so drunk. I take a few minutes to collect myself, then he emerges from the bathroom.

"You should go," he says. "I'll call you."

I'm not sure if I believe him. I find the exit. I'm still wobbly, but I make it to my car. I wake up the next morning in my bed, not sure exactly how I got there.

It's been a week and John has not called or responded to my texts. *So much for Aruba.* I've been duped. Why am I such an idiot who gives it up right away? He barely had to try. He got everything he wanted, and I got nothing. Would I have agreed to sex with him if there wasn't the allure of being his traveling sugar baby? *Fuck no.* My throat swells like I need to vomit whenever I think about him. Is this what he does to girls? What an asshole.

I got *got*. I'm just going to pretend this never happened, no one needs to know. Just like I didn't tell anyone about Jack when I was fourteen, or about the money Kris scammed me out of. It's easier to bury it. The best thing I can do now is get back on SA, a little wiser, and try my hand again. *Don't sleep with someone on the first date. Noted.*

Chapter 8

Second Date

Ironically, my second date is also a man named John. John #2. He's twice my age and lives in Phoenix. His profile has a mirror pic with only his torso, a reddish tan with gray chest hair. We chat on the phone for a bit before he decides to come out to Vegas for the night just to meet me. His voice is raspy, and I let him do most of the talking.

"Don't text me," he says. "I have a flip phone, and I don't text."

I pick out a strapless dress and pink velvet pumps, remembering what Christine told me: always wear heels to meet a sugar daddy. He wants me to meet him at Wynn. I was at this resort a couple months before for Encore Beach Club. I got blackout drunk, lost my cell phone, and locked myself out of my house. This is my second time on the property, and I'm itching for a comeback.

I find him at a bar near the valet. "John?" He swivels around in his seat, but his gray curls stay put. "So great to finally meet you."

"Are you ready for dinner?" he asks, tossing back his bourbon or whatever.

I take his arm over his Tommy Bahama shirt, and his muscle is surprisingly more cut than I anticipate. We walk down to Lakeside, a seafood restaurant with a pond and a corny show that plays on the hour where an animatronic frog sings Frank Sinatra. We sit outside next to a glass case of live lobster that the waitstaff wheel around so patrons can pick their own meal. John #2 gets red wine with ice and swirls the contents of his glass.

"I only like red wine when it's ice cold, and I know some people think that's a faux pas."

"Oh, I'm not one of them." I smirk. I didn't know that was a thing, but I'm learning. *No red wine with ice, got it.*

John #2's steak arrives, and he pokes it. He cuts it down the center and complains to the waiter. "Well, this here is medium. I ordered medium rare." He points at the perfectly pink rib eye on his plate. "Would you say this is medium, or medium rare?"

The waiter moves his head to get a few angles. "Medium rare, sir. Is it to your liking?"

"Medium rare huh? If you say so." John #2 adjusts the plate, defeated.

He saws off a few bites, then pushes it away in favor of the breadbasket. I let him talk while I smile, nod, and laugh at the faintest hint of a cue. I gulp my wine and order another, the first one warm from sitting out in the late summer heat. When the bill comes, the waiter asks how everything was.

"Well, the steak was overcooked, so I didn't eat it," John #2 says.

"I'm so sorry to hear that," the waiter answers, genuinely surprised. "Let me take that off your bill."

John #2 cracks a weak smile for the first time when the adjusted tab arrives. I'm still not finished with my wine.

"Bring it with you, we're getting out of here," he directs, and I follow.

Outside the restaurant there are a few kids going backwards down the escalator, shrill screams as the metal stairs ascend to their delight.

We dodge them and John grumbles, "Keep your kids in check!"

Okay, grandpa. He bugs. I take another gulp of my wine and shrug it off. It's becoming evident why he pays for dates. Wait… *am I even getting paid for this?* We never discussed money.

We meander to the craps tables. I've never played before, but I'm a quick study: blow on the dice and throw them when instructed, but not too hard. Call it beginner's luck, but we end up winning over ten grand. By that time, I'm way too drunk to drive so we go back to his suite, and I promptly fall asleep.

I wake up in a sea of billowy white bedding to the jingle of John #2 pushing a room service cart and stationing it by the window. My pink pumps and dress are still intact, having slept atop the duvet.

"Good morning," he greets me all chipper. "Do you want some OJ?" He pours himself some coffee. "I left something in your purse."

My head is pounding. I gather my wits and walk across the rather large room to the entry table where my black Steve Madden bag sits. Inside is a wad of hundreds. I don't count, but it's clearly more cash than I've ever possessed, at least a thousand dollars.

"Thank you," I say, my voice cracking.

Next to the cash is my spiral of birth control, the pill I forgot to take yesterday. I can't take it now. I'd throw it up for sure. I maintain my composure and join John #2 on the sectional for some orange juice. I chug the small glass and he starts caressing my leg, kissing my thigh. The reality sets in that I might have to fuck him for the money.

"I'm on my period," I spew, the first excuse I can think of. He stops, visibly off put. My lie worked.

"Let's take a shower," he says. A shower sounds good, but I don't want to have sex with him.

Not entirely sure how I'm going to navigate the logistics, I agree. He turns on the water and I get undressed. I meet him under the rainfall showerhead, and he kisses me. Then he puts his hand on the back of my neck and slowly pushes me down onto the shower bench. I know that move.

John grips his erection, "Do you want to help me with this?"

I most certainly do not, but I've found myself in a compromising position. The prospect of John regularly filling my purse with hundreds helps me to open my mouth. I wince as he crams it against the inside of my cheek, doing the work for me. It doesn't last long, and the cleanup is easy. A wad of cash for a blow job? Not a bad deal.

I put on a robe and sit on the couch. John #2 has to catch his flight back to Arizona, but he tells me I can order more room service. He kisses me goodbye and disappears behind the soft-close door. I leaf through the menu, but I can't eat anything right now. Not sure if it's the hangover or the misguided attempt at sex work, but I'm nauseous. I stare out the rose-tinted window and take off my own rose-tinted glasses. What just happened? I run to the bathroom and purge. I hear my phone vibrate in my purse. It's a text from another POT, which I learned from Christine is slang for a potential sugar daddy. This one also wants to meet at Wynn. What are the odds? My clothes are dirty, and my sensibilities bruised. I go home and regroup.

Once home, I realize I've forgotten my watch in the room. I call John to see if he can help me get it back, but no answer. I count the money, one thousand five hundred dollars. A fair trade, I guess. He doesn't call me back, but I'm hopeful he might. I consider it a win either way. Now, off to meet the next daddy. Maybe I can get another grand out of him.

Chapter 9

The Trust Fund Guy

I head back to Wynn to meet Jeff. He was persistent on the phone. He told me he's young and different from the other guys on the site. Well, I've been on all of two dates: first one I was swindled and the other, basically an escort. Jeff doesn't send me a picture, and I have no idea who I'm meeting. The range of possibilities makes my heart palpitate. It's a gamble, just like last night at the craps table. Only now I'm gambling with my body, wagering my health, safety, and maybe my sanity. I'm one for two at this point, so I chase. I could be riding a streak!

Jeff tells me in a text that he's at the casual restaurant, Society. The dining room is empty and there is only one person at the bar. It must be him. I touch his shoulder to get his attention. He turns, then wipes his fingers on the napkin draped over his pale pink shorts. At 6'5, he towers when he stands to greet me, going in for a double cheek kiss. How European. He is in fact younger than most men on SA, only twenty-nine, eight years older than me. I order a club sandwich and the physical chemistry is instant. He tells me about his new app idea for retail shopping. Why would someone want to shop for clothes on their phone? I feign interest.

"By the way, my name isn't Jeff," he confesses. "It's Scott." He pulls out his black AMEX and gives it to the bartender. "What's the scar from?" he asks, pointing to his own chin, to the crumbs he doesn't know are there.

I know what he means. I have a scar on my cheek, from the right corner of my lips as though a fishhook might have caught me. I used to make that joke when I was younger to get ahead of the teasing. The real story is an accident with the family dog when I was only three years old. My dad was supposed to be watching me while chipping golf balls in the backyard. Our golden retriever-lab mix took off after one of the balls, running over my little toddler face. Her claw tore the skin between my chin and cheek on the right side resulting in 50 stitches. We didn't have money for a plastic surgeon, so I've been left with a noticeable but not disfiguring scar. I rarely think about it.

"Oh, it's from a dog." I say, touching the skin.

"Damn," he says. "You'd be perfect without that." His phone starts buzzing and he takes the call. He exchanges a few words with the caller. Says to me, "Do you want to go to Wet Republic?"

"I don't have a swimsuit."

"I'll get you one." He takes the bait.

"Okay then, sure," I agree.

At the very least, I'll get a new bathing suit out of this dalliance. A shop at the Wynn has single pieces starting at around a hundred dollars. I find a white bikini with brass rings at the hips. I try it on while Scott talks on his phone.

"What do you think?" I twirl.

"That's hot."

He barely looks. Does he really think I'm hot? I take my haul to the register, and he swipes his black card without looking at the amount, still mid-conversation on his phone. The total is just under four hundred. I thank him, though I'm not sure he cares. We hop in an SUV for hire outside the Tower Suites and head to MGM. Despite Scott not showing me any affection, I am in material girl heaven. I could get used to this.

We arrive at the cabana where there are about twenty people, mostly from NYC like him. I try to make nice with the girls. Aloof, influencer types cling to Saint Laurent clutches. They spot my Steve Madden purse and are subsequently unimpressed. I get the feeling they know something about Scott that I don't. After a few hours of dancing and Dom Perignon, the pool is closing, and the group wants to go to dinner. We pile into an Excursion stretch limo waiting outside the club. I get in first with Scott, and the car fills up. I take the opportunity to sit on Scott's lap, making room for one more. I think it will give me a chance to be physical but regret it when I see his discomfort. My head is up against the ceiling, and he's squished. I'm the tacky girl no one knows forcing the guy paying the tab to be uncomfortable. He's visibly irritated. I blew it. The short ride feels like an eternity. We get dropped off back at the Wynn, and I assume I'm going to dinner with the group.

"I'll call you later," Scott says, planting a wet kiss on my lips in the lobby.

The other girls whisk him away as I process what's happening. Ditched again. I take a deep breath and watch the group walk off, holding the hurt. My buzz gives me the strength not to cry right there on the casino floor. Spending an evening with that pretentious bunch isn't what I want, and I'm already getting a hangover so I'm glad to go home.

Back in my bed, I turn up the ringer on my phone before closing my eyes. Somehow, I can't shake the feeling of rejection. Am I just not what these men are looking for? On a site like SeekingArrangement, I'm sure they have options. He said he'd call me later. He doesn't.

Chapter 10

The Mexican

My date tonight is with a daddy from Mexico who's on a business trip. His profile says his name is Hector, married with no pictures. He calls me in the morning.

"I want to go somewhere off the Strip, I can't have any of my coworkers see us."

He has a thick accent and a slight lisp but seems nice enough. I suggest Ferraro's, an Italian restaurant behind the Hard Rock. It's low key and the food is incredible. Jasmin and I like to go there for happy hour. I get to the restaurant first and grab a table in the main dining room. In walks a tall Latino with a hairline to be proud of. He's a little heavy set and wearing a black suit jacket and pants, no tie. I wave when I see him. After eyeballing every corner of the restaurant, he comes tableside and bends down for a kiss on the cheek.

"Do you mind if we sit somewhere else?" he asks and looks around the room again, keeping his head down.

"Sure, wherever you like."

He has the waiter move us to a table in the corner where he can watch the door but not be seen by other patrons. There are only a handful of people here, but I understand. I don't want his wife to come for me either. She could be a Cartel boss for all I know. Hector lets me do most of the talking, asks me questions about my interests and goals. He laughs at my jokes and lets me order for the table. Beef carpaccio, gnocchi and branzino with a Pinot Noir because it's the only wine I like. We finish our meal, and he asks if I want to go back to his room.

"Where are you staying?" I ask nonchalantly. It's a loaded question because you can tell a lot about someone with this info. Wynn or Bellagio = rich. Cosmo or Venetian = thinks they're rich. MGM or Mirage = doesn't know any better. Anything else, probably just a normie looking for a cheap vacation.

"Treasure Island, I think? It's from my company." Yikes. He gets a pass because it's a group booking.

"Sure, I can drive us."

Hector gets into my 2010 Dodge Caliber, and I drive us a couple miles to Treasure Island.

"Can you drop me off here and meet me upstairs? I'll text you my room number," he asks when we get to the parking garage.

I park the car and wait a few minutes. The text comes through. I head to his room. I'm going to ask him for fifteen hundred. That's what I got last time I did something like this, and it almost made the act worth it. I need to make my demands clear, no more mistakes. In the hall outside his room, I slow my pace and take a few deep breaths before tapping on the door. *It's not that serious*, I tell myself to soothe. The room is dark, one bed, and an armchair in the corner. I chat with him, dripping sweetness. Then we get down to brass tacks.

"So, how much do you think you can give me?" I begin the negotiation.

"How much do you need?"

"I'm thinking like fifteen hundred."

"*Fifteen hundred?*" he echoes, sticker shocked.

"Well, that's what my other daddy gives me." I bat my eyelashes and look at my feet, red toenails in my peep toe pumps.

"Okay, I have to go to the ATM. You'll wait here?"

"That's fine," I reply, a little surprised it worked. Ten minutes later he's back in the room and cracks open his brown leather wallet.

"I was only able to get eight hundred, I have a daily limit. But I can send you the rest tomorrow." Hector's hand is trembling as he hands me the cash.

"I guess that's okay," I respond, trying to show my disappointment.

"I'm sorry."

I like his sincerity, so I weigh my options. I can act like a brat and demand he get me some chips or something or choose to believe him and go through with it. The latter seems more lucrative, so I sit down on the bed and rub the spot beside me and motion for him to come hither.

I notice his sweat soaked collar as he sits beside me, the firm old mattress creaking. He kisses me tenderly; his lips are soft and it's clear he hasn't been touched intimately in a long time. I almost feel bad for him. I suck him off briefly before he grabs a condom and climbs on top. Two minutes later he finishes, and I sense it's my cue to leave, winnings in tow.

The next day Hector asks for my banking details and wires me five hundred dollars. It should be seven, but I don't mention it. Consider it a discount. It's always best to stay sweet with these men, even when they misstep. That's how I'll keep him sweet on me.

CHAPTER 11

THE MILK DUD

I'm at the bottom of my savings when I meet Vince, a forty-two-year-old business owner living in Miami. He sends me a picture privately because, like most men on SA, he doesn't have a profile picture. He's six foot two and looks like he knows how to eat. He's convinced that I hook up with a ton of guys and makes it clear he wants to be the only man in my life. That's fine with me, makes things easier. That is, if he's able to give me what I'm looking for. We're both a little desperate, him for companionship and me for a lifestyle change. After a few late-night phone calls, Vince is smitten and wants to meet in person. A supposedly well-heeled man unable to find a local match in Florida begs the question: Why fly two-thousand miles for a woman?

Simply put, Vince wants to fuck hot young girls. I'm guessing he's not attractive or affluent enough to pull any in Miami, so he's using SA. He truly hopes to find a wife half his age. I think this makes him "one of the good ones." We're a pair of opportunists masquerading as romantics. Two peas in a pod. Vince wants a beautiful girl to be enamored with him, so I am, or rather I pretend to be.

My strategy is to fake interest until I figure out whether he's rich and, more importantly, generous. What's expendable income if he's not willing to spend it on my affection? If he is, I'll find out what his life is missing and try to fill the void. If I'm going to put off getting a real job after graduation, I need to secure the bag soon. I send him sexy photos and good morning texts to butter him up before his visit. He lands in Vegas early on a Friday in October and sends me a text. He says he's shopping for me at Saks.

I've never even *been* to Saks. This guy seems like the real deal, and I do not want to fuck it up. Vince is staying at Vdara, the only resort on The Strip without a casino floor. That evening, we meet at the lobby bar nestled amid orchids and marble floors. They pump scented oxygen into these places, this time gardenia, supposedly it makes people stay longer. It's a scent that reminds me of my grandmother who taught me about flora and fauna. What will she think of me now? I try not to get bogged down with such thoughts, especially not when Vince is waiting, my glass of wine poured.

"You're handsome," I say, trying not to study his appearance the way I usually do on a first date.

He blushes. I notice his sagging jowls, my gaze trailing to the back of his neck as he turns and takes a sip. His neck rolls look like stacked hot-dogs, his bald head like a giant Milk Dud. I take a big gulp of my wine. Vince smiles, revealing a small chip on his front left tooth.

"You're prettier in person," he says, smacking his lips.

Vince is not prettier in person. The pictures he sent were definitely taken several years ago, back when he had more hair and less belly fat. I'm not usually into men with this physique, but I need to drop my physical standards with these sugar daddies. Plus, it's easy to give his appearance a pass when there are designer duds awaiting me. He mistakes my enthusiasm for the gifts as excitement about meeting him. I allow it, flipping my hair and giggling all the way to the bank. Without the tokens, I wouldn't be so charming.

"Let's go up to the room and I'll show you what I got for you."

He throws back his rum and coke, leaves a few twenties on the bar. This is my *Pretty Woman* pipedream. Dollar signs are spinning in my head. I wonder how much he spent on me. I'm high on the anticipation, or maybe it's just the weed I smoked before I came. Money for me means safety. When my mom filed for bankruptcy in 2008, any feelings I had of financial security disappeared. I've never quite gotten it back.

During the elevator ride, Vince touches the small of my back, waiting to see my reaction. I don't have one, as I'm used to this sort of contact. Men I don't even know think this is an appropriate place to touch me, and it's not worth my time to tell them otherwise. He moves his hand down to my butt and gives it a good squeeze. I grimace.

"You've got a great ass," he says and grunts.

He leads me to a corner suite and pushes open the door. I see two Saks bags and a black garment bag on the couch. He unzips it, slowly.

"I hope you like it," he says, holding up a black sequined dress. I certainly do. It's short and sexy and partially transparent. "And I got you these." He uncovers a Jimmy Choo box.

Is this my Carrie Bradshaw moment? I open the box, revealing a black and gold strappy pair of heels, a size too small. I try them anyway but end up feeling more like Cinderella's ugly stepsister than *Sex and the City*. There is no chance I'm shoving my wide and untried piggies into these delicate shoes. I feel like an ogre. How was I supposed to know designer shoes are made for elves? Apparently, you always go a size up.

"We'll go back to Saks tomorrow and exchange them," Vince says.

I love that idea because it means we'll be going shopping together. Fortunately, I brought shoes I can wear. The dress is a little tight on my autumn body, but he did great. I truly love it.

We have dinner at Aria. I eat like a bird. I'm already stuffed into this dress. I figure he doesn't want a girl with an appetite, so I peck on some sashimi and drink my Pinot Noir.

Afterwards he gets a table at Hakkasan for Steve Aoki where the minimum spend is two grand. According to my careful calculations, Vince is indeed rich enough to advance to the next level. Cue the slot machine and cash register noises. *Cha-ching.* I summon a few friends and ask them to bring party favors, figuring a pinch of molly might help me relax into a little intimacy. The table next to us is a bachelor party full of attractive men closer to my age. Is it bad to wish I was with them instead? This is what I wanted. I pour myself another vodka cranberry. The music is so loud I get away with not making any conversation, plus Christine and couple of my friends are here as a buffer. Naturally there's an unspoken understanding that I'm staying the night with Vince. It's my duty as a sugar baby. And I must deliver, despite not being remotely attracted to him, a small detail I need to forget. I'm on my period, so we'll see what happens. Does that excuse me from sex? We head back to the room, and I'll find out.

"I don't want our first time to be like this," I contest as he unzips my dress and fondles me. "I'm on my period."

Vince climbs on top of me, his gut pinning me, and goes in for a kiss. I don't have much choice at this point. Once again, I'm too drunk to care. His hand reaches into my underwear, and he attempts to fondle me, but instead finds my tampon. Before I can object, he grabs the string and yanks it out, flinging it through the air. I feel a sting like he scratched me down there, and I protest with a whimper. "Ouch!"

Vince runs his mouth on my leg with a voracity that freezes me. He won't be having any excuses. He's going to take what he wants. The fact that I'm here in this dress is consent. His body is suffocating, and his dick is so small I barely feel it. I wait for him to finish. Once he does, I recover my blood-soaked tampon from the floor. In the bathroom I pause at my reflection and stare back, disgusted. Was that worth it? To be determined.

The next morning, we go to Saks to return the shoes which takes my mind off the abhorrent sex. Now that we've fucked, I hope it opens him up to opening his wallet even more. I drive us to the Fashion Show Mall in my silver Dodge Caliber. *Don't you want to buy me a Range Rover, daddy?* Last time I was here, it was with Jasmin and Kris before he bought me the bathing suits. I ended up paying for them in the end when he scammed me. How the tables have turned ... right?

"If they don't have my size maybe I can get a watch instead," I hint on the escalator from the parking garage.

"I want you to get shoes," Vince says.

I try not to let his pointed comment ruin it for me. I'm thrilled to be at Saks for the first time. I breathe in the exorbitance, or maybe it's Paco Rabanne. There's a spritz of tension in the air. I stay silent until we reach the footwear section. They don't have my size in the Jimmy Choos. Black Saint Laurent Tribute Sandals catch my eye, and I show the display to Vince.

"What about these?"

"Those are hooker shoes," he says.

"Your point?" I say, considering I sort of am one. Vince is not amused.

"Let's see if they have these."

He grabs a closed toed Tribute Pump, an equally hooker-ish shoe if you ask me. They have my size in stock, but the style does not suit my ugly stepsister-shaped foot. I barely squeeze my pinkies in, never mind walking. I cram my feet into them anyway and trot down the aisle like a fucking Clydesdale.

"Are there any others you like?" I wonder aloud.

"Those are the ones. They look so hot." Vince grins like a kid.

He starts playing on his phone. He's made his decision, and now he's ready to go. It's less complicated if I just agree to the toe crushers. The shoes he wants are better than no shoes at all, and I suppose he reserves that right as the one with the money. I get what I get and *like it*. He gets the fantasy. Who's getting the better end of the deal? I exchange glares with the salesperson and recede.

"We'll take the eight and a half," I mutter, sliding the box across the counter.

Vince pays the price difference, and I make sure to keep the receipt. This is an eight-hundred-dollar pair of shoes, but it doesn't feel as good as I thought it would. Do I even want these shoes? I'm not sure. Maybe I just want other people to know I have them. Jasmin and Christine are going to be so jealous.

Vince leaves the next morning, so I figure it's the right time to negotiate. I'm broke as a joke and in desperate need of funds. The first item on the list is my dead tooth. Just like Maureen Ponderosa before me, I have a dead tooth. Mine is the result of a bike accident when I was eight that knocked out my front teeth. After the root canal, my front left tooth remained slightly dark. I tell Vince how uncomfortable it makes me now that I'm turning twenty-two and it's still not fixed, but I don't have the money to pay for the crown even with my insurance. He agrees to send me the money. What I don't tell him is that I also complained to my biological father about the dental fees, and he graciously offered to pay for it as well. *Bio dad and daddy for the win.* That will help me recoup that sports betting loss and get back to baseline with my funds.

Vince heads to the airport first thing. I pretend to sleep while he packs. He gives me a peck on the cheek and leaves. I can finally breath. I hang back and order room service and take some pictures of myself by the corner windows for my Instagram. I text Vince my banking information. The next day he transfers the money.

Over the next few weeks, Vince and I talk every day and make plans to see each other again in Miami. Even from a distance, he's controlling and constantly worried I'm seeing other guys. Between keeping in constant contact, work, and school, I don't have time to fuck around. Plus, I don't want to screw things up. Vince is my golden ticket.

The plan is simple. I still have a semester of credits left to earn my degree, but Vince wants to do some traveling soon. His grand idea is a long vacation, each stop progressing our latitude until we circumnavigate the globe. He legit wants to take me on a trip around the world! *Eeek!* He's letting me choose the destinations as a graduation present. My knight in shining Armani. I had applied for my passport last week!

I spend my free time researching and comparing locales, decide the best route. Our trip means my degree will be on hold for at least a semester. That worries me, but I don't want to squander the opportunity. Christine and Shayla agreed, I should go for it. Most girls never get a chance like this. Greece, Japan, and Hawaii seem like a perfect excuse for putting school on hold. The university will be here when I get back.

The only thing standing in the way is my job at the cock cage company. Vince loathes me being in the sex industry, so he pressures me to quit. Leaving my job is the only way I'll be able to travel. He assures me he'll take care of me financially. I put in my two weeks.

For our next rendezvous, Vince wants to show me a weekend in Miami. He books me on Spirit, and I take the redeye. Vince picks me up in his Maserati GranTurismo, gunmetal with red leather interior. He smells like coffee and sweat as he goes in for a moist kiss. Everything is moist in Florida.

The sun is shining and so is my attitude. I snap a selfie in the passenger seat with the Maserati logo behind me while he fills up the tank. I asked Vince to get me some weed. He had a friend acquire a vape pen and some wax. He calls it "hash." We drive to South Beach, and I take long drags from my new pen, blow it out the window. I see my reflection in the rear-view mirror. *This could be your life,* I remind her.

Vince booked us a corner suite at Eden Roc. I guess that's his thing. I'm jet lagged, so when night rolls around I can't sleep. Vince is too tired to fuck, so I get the night off. He snores while I listen to the party in the hotel room next door. I smoke my pen on the balcony for a while and listen to the crowd. I even consider making an appearance over there. Vince would *kill* me. Instead, I call security. I hate myself for making the call, partially because I wish I was with them, but I'm a light sleeper. I peer through the peephole as security kicks the partiers out. Victory is mine.

Vince and I spend the next day by the beach and at the jacuzzi munching on poolside snacks. While I'm in the hot tub, he heads to the restroom. It crosses my mind that he likes to take a long time in the bathroom, but I hope it won't become an issue. I wait, then text and call with no response. I didn't bring a key, and I don't think my name is on the room. It's nearly an hour before he returns.

"Where were you?" I ask, thinking no one takes that long in the bathroom. "It's been over an hour."

"I told you. I went to the bathroom."

Now the trade-off is clear: Vince gets to disappear and do whatever he damn well pleases in exchange for his generosity. Tolerance on my part is mandatory. *Quid pro quo.* Vince has never been married but has a teenage son in Michigan, allegedly the result of a one-night stand. He was engaged once but never made it to the altar. He boasted about the eighty-thousand-dollar ring he bought her, so expensive he had a decoy made. Despite the prospect of a fat rock, I don't want to marry Vince. People believe what they want to believe, and Vince believes I'm really into him. I'm out of his league by a mile, and the discrepancy is glaring. Men like him choose to overlook the discernible truth in exchange for intimacy, no matter how forced.

After dinner Vince drives to Wall, a club at the W Hotel. We push through the hoard of partiers, shrieks of laughter, and general hoots of merriment to the bar. I press up against his belly, with no room to move.

Vince could easily be my dad but is obviously my daddy. Why else would someone like me be with someone like him? I can't hold shame about the men I'm with, they'll notice eventually. I'm taking home the bag, so I need to get accustomed to looking and feeling like an escort. I mean, I sort of am … or am I? The question is too much to unpack. I last about fifteen minutes before telling Vince I want to head out. There are too many hot guys here and I'm tired of looking at them while standing next to my Milk Dud of a man.

The next day Vince makes a detour to the University of Miami campus. As we drive through Coral Gables, he stares out the window, nostalgic in a slightly pathetic way.

"This is where I used to go to class," he says and points. "And that's where you can get your master's."

My what? I have no plans of prolonging my studies and I'm not even done with my bachelor's. Plus, I want to be a writer, not a student. My future is already mapped in his mind, and my desires take a back seat. He envisions a future where I stay in school and remain a college girl for the duration of his delusion. We stop by a U merch store where he picks out an orange and green crop top for me. He dresses me in what he wants, and I am grateful for the honor. *Yes, sir. Thank you, sir.*

He drives me back to the airport for my evening flight. The trip was an overall success, despite not getting any gifts besides the wax pen and the U shirt. After the trip to Saks, I thought we'd at least hit the mall. Instead, we hit the gator park for an airboat ride and nature show. My twenty-second birthday is in a couple weeks where I'm sure to reap some sugar baby rewards.

I turn my phone on after the flight and see a notification Vince sent me regarding our agreed upon fifteen hundred dollars for my bills, a stipulation of me quitting my job. I agreed to be more available for him and he's paying for it. Seeing the transaction makes me furrow my brow. Am I concerned for myself? Does this mean he owns me? Thankfully he's thousands of miles away, so the grip isn't too tight.

The following month, he takes me to Key West for my birthday. He picks me up from the airport in a black Silverado truck this time. My flight was delayed four hours and I barely slept, but I'm also just not enthused to see him. It really does feel like work, despite being a vacation. He's a chore.

"Where's the Maserati?" I inquire after the requisite hug and kiss. That was half the fun of being with him last time I was here.

"We've got a long drive. A truck is better," he says, and chucks my purple hard-shell suitcase in the back. It clamors.

Since it's my birthday I figured he would do something special like pay for a helicopter ride or private jet. A long drive hadn't been in my scope of possibilities. I stare out the window, feeling like I'm going to stay with my dad for the weekend. The vibe is obligatory. The Overseas Highway is just like the name suggests, a bridge built over the water between the isles. We ride on the ocean, across infinite turquoise waves, sun glistening off the surface of the water. I understand why he likes the drive. It's ethereal. The experience is extraordinary, but I just wish it was with someone else.

He booked us at the Hyatt in a two-bedroom corner suite (of course) with a kitchen and panoramic terrace overlooking the coast, fully romantic. I unpack a few things before dinner.

"I brought the shoes," I say, holding up the silk dust bag, thinking he'll be pleased.

"You shouldn't wear them here. It's not that kind of place."

I ignore his advice and wear them anyway. I soon realize we're not in Miami anymore. How was I supposed to know Key West is essentially a jungle? I stumble over uneven sidewalks to a dive bar. When I notice the scuffed soles, my heart sinks. My misstep caused irreparable damage, but I don't mention that he was right.

The next morning, I cook breakfast. He's touched. It's my birthday, and his grand idea is to rent a boat for the day. That could be fun, right? I could get some great pictures for my Instagram on the bow of something sporty. My expectations for a luxury speedboat are quickly thwarted when I see the canoe Vince reserved for us. It's a fishing boat with one small seat. It smells like tuna guts. Dismayed and embittered, I reluctantly board the S.S. *Disappointment*. This is how he treats me on my birthday?

I sit in the little chair, and we put out of the marina. Vince looks like a fat captain save a hoe. We cruise for about forty-five minutes before coming across a small, wooded island. Vince drops anchor and I jump out for a swim. We didn't bring any floaties, so I cling to the life preserver attached by a rope. It's nice to get a break from Vince, floating adrift in the choppy waters. My face is crystallized with salt, my lips are chapped and burnt, and I am famished. Of course we didn't bring food. Some celebration.

Back at the Hyatt, it's finally time for the moment I've been waiting for: my gift. Vince digs through his bag and presents me with a small Burberry box. I gasp with joy; thank god he was listening. For a brief moment suspended in time, I am met with the spoils of my emotional labor. All the times I bit my tongue and held back my sassy remarks, replacing them with sweet platitudes. It all comes down to this moment. Real sugar baby shit. Inside is an oversized, ivory face watch with a cream leather strap. I asked for a big watch, and he delivered. I swoon over it, trying it on and looking in the mirror. I plant a big kiss on his lips and wrap my arms around his neck.

"Thank you so much."

As I stare at the round face and it stares back at me, I feel it's missing something. The gift is nice, but I sort of expected more. He spent thousands on me in Las Vegas. Now on my birthday he has a chance to really spoil me, and I get the fishing boat from hell and an accessory? Don't get me wrong, I appreciate the sentiment, but it seems ordinary after the luxe weekend back home. I assume he's getting tapped out. Maybe he's not as rich or generous as I thought. *Be grateful*, I remind myself. He'll loosen the purse strings eventually.

The next morning it's time to check out. I packed my things last night, so I'd be ready. It's overcast and the wind is whipping through my hair as I wait for Vince by the door, tapping my foot like an impatient wife. He takes me straight to departures and I barely make my flight. At the airport I get a call from my father, my biological daddy, wishing me a late happy birthday. He says he can never remember which day it is.

As I'm gassing up my car after work the following day, I realize I'm low on money. I text Vince to ask about the next installment of my allowance. My entitlement shows, and Vince doesn't respond. For days. He won't take my calls, doesn't answer my texts. I start to panic. I quit my job for him, and now *this*?

The glaring truth is I will never love him and am blatantly using him. Only I thought we were both in on the ruse. Did he truly think I would love him? I text him probably a hundred times. I leave voicemails, crying and inconsolable. He abandoned me. Full ghost. How am I going to pay my bills now?

Not only did I quit my job, but I never picked my final semester of courses for graduation because of our travel plans. By the time I log on to select classes, everything is full and the deadline for financial aid has long passed. Returning to school next semester is not an option. And I flunked sugaring 101. Today's lesson: never let him feel used. Once the facade is compromised, the whole structure crumbles. Vince and I crashed and burned. For him, it was the money he'd lost. My situation went from glamor to dire in a blink. That's the risk I took on SeekingArrangement. I gambled with my future and lost.

This is the first time I've put my trust in a man and been so phenomenally let down. The feeling is familiar, an injustice I can't quite place. I think of Aaron, who wound me up in a web of lies. And Kris, who promised the ticket was a winner. My parents let me down, too. During my early years, they told me they were saving money for my college tuition. I thought I'd be one of the lucky ones, getting a debt-free start to life. The reality was revealed to me by my mother after a bottle of wine when I was about eight years old. "You don't have a college fund," she'd told me. "We spent it on the motor home. You like taking vacations, don't you?" They got rid of the old Coachman a year later in the divorce.

Heaving and bawling after being ghosted by Vince, I drive to my mom's house for support. She's keenly aware of my escapades and knows I was dating a man twenty years my senior. I even showed her a picture before I left for my birthday trip.

"Why don't you call the woman who offered you an interview a few months ago?"

She rubs my back gently. I sit sobbing on her stairs with my face in my hands. It's not a bad idea. Through tears I scroll for the text message, having forgotten about it. *What was her name...*

[Dec 6, 2013, 3:52 PM]
Me: Hi Jackie. Are you still looking for help?

CHAPTER 12

HAPPY GRADUATION

Fresh out of options and a few credits short of my degree, kickstarting my life with a big girl job is my road to redemption. I need this job. More importantly, I need money. At UNLV we're allowed to walk for graduation before completing all our credits, which seems like a good idea. I won't receive a diploma, but the optics are convincing. I pull out my iPhone 4 in the parking garage before the ceremony and see an email from Jackie. It's an offer letter for Public Relations Coordinator with InfoStream Group, Inc, the parent company of SeekingArrangement. I'll be making $35,000 a year, which is more than I've ever made before, full benefits included.

This is the American dream. My own Horatio Alger story, like Hunter S. Thompson says. Even though I don't have the diploma to prove it, I'm still a journalism major. I take a deep inhale. It smells like rain, and I hear the soft patter on the parking lot. This is the perfect news to share with my family after I walk. But there's a knot in my gut. I'm reminded of something my cousin, Nancy, mentioned about the website that rubbed me the wrong way.

Nancy is a sex worker. She's a couple years older than me, I'm twenty-two and she's twenty-four. Last week I visited her in San Diego and stayed at her place in Little Italy. She'd asked me for help with her website. It features pictures of her in lingerie, pigtails, bending over. One caption read: *Have you ever wanted to fuck the girl next-door?* She also has a profile on Backpage, a notorious classifieds website for prostitution.

The first time I was introduced to Backpage was through Nancy's ad. I remember looking over my mother's shoulder as she gasped in disbelief at the link my uncle forwarded. There was eighteen-year-old Nancy, scantily clad and sickly thin posed on her hands and knees in fishnet stockings, priced at three hundred an hour. I wanted to believe that wasn't the girl I grew up with, but the pixel proof was there.

When she invited me to stay in her guest room, I jumped at the chance to reconnect with my estranged childhood best friend. It was great to see her, but her appearance struck me. Listless with pale skin, like when Megan Fox becomes the hungry demon in *Jennifer's Body*. I found someone who is now a far cry from the firecracker I grew up with. I told her I got a new job, working for a website called SeekingArrangement.

"I know that site," she'd told me, raising her thin eyebrows. "You should be careful, there's no reviews on there. Some men who get kicked off Backpage go to SeekingArrangement."

It makes sense, SA is all about anonymity. I'm acutely aware of the type of men on there, but I'm not working for them ... right? My bad experiences on the site were the result of my own naivety. Since those indiscretions were my fault, it would reflect poorly on me to let anyone know what happened. In a way, I'm doubling down by joining the team. It will afford me a sort of plausible deniability. Who would work for a company that caused them to be exploited for sex? *Me, I guess.* Somehow, this feels like the path of least resistance. Like faking my graduation, faking interest in these sugar daddies, and faking orgasms. It's always easier to placate and keep things copesetic. Sun setting, I force a swallow and step out of the car. It's showtime.

PART TWO: 2014

Age: 22
Playlist: Kygo, The Chainsmokers, Ellie Goulding
TV: *The Walking Dead, How to Get Away with Murder, Orange is the New Black*
Favorite pastime: Going on dates I don't pay for

Chapter 13

Sugar Baby Schools

Jackie told me I could start the job when everyone got back after the holidays, but I insisted on December 30th as my first day. I need to get my bank account back up. My second day was New Year's Eve. Only a handful of people were in the office. Jackie brought in five bottles of cheap champagne, and we toasted with plastic cups.

I rummage through my clothes hangers like a filing cabinet. Since working retail, I keep it color coordinated, but nothing is screaming "career woman." I've already worn my four best business looks, so I opt for a repeat of my interview outfit, a knit sweater dress, and head into the office.

SA HQ is an open concept space with Facebook blue walls, gray concrete floors, white desks, and exposed HVAC. The space and employees are divided by department. Development, marketing, and customer support. It's almost all men, and I get the feeling most of them know their way around a computer, but maybe not around a woman. They keep to themselves.

"We have a big pitch coming up," Jackie says as I get settled.

She takes a sip from the drink on her desk – a mason jar containing green juice with a thick straw – then sets the cup beside her planner. Noticing her calendar and notes are exposed, she flips the pages over.

"Okay," I say, setting my bag so Jackie can't see the frayed edges on the strap. "Sounds interesting."

She breaks down the PR strategy for me. The biggest pitch of the year for SA is about sugar babies attending college. Around here they call it by a single word: schools. Short for "sugar baby schools," it's a ranking of the numbers of sugar baby students at major universities and colleges. It seems like Jackie's prized project, a juicy story that made headlines the last two years. She's gotten dozens of placements in major outlets, and the site had a noticeable bump in member sign-ups. She thinks it can be even bigger this year. She says January is the perfect time to send the pitch because reporters and producers are looking for a substantial, ratings-making piece right before sweeps in February. A story like sugar babies paying for expensive university tuition with funds provided by sugar daddies. It's a tough economy, especially in [insert city here]!

"How do we know where they go to college?" I ask, perusing a CNN article on the topic she sent me from last year. It reads:

> While some may compare the practice to prostitution or question the morality of trading money and gifts for affection, the people who use these sites contend that they're merely a conduit for both parties getting what they want.

Both parties getting what they want … I reread the last words and overlay them onto my own sugar dalliances. The men got what they wanted. But did I get what I wanted? Not exactly. Not yet anyway. I'm in the market for a rich boyfriend. Hopefully working here gives me a leg up.

"College sugar babies get free premium membership if they sign up with their university email," Jackie says. "Like how Amazon and Microsoft have student discounts."

The .edu email addresses show us where they go to college. There are a lot of college sugar babies already, but she juices the numbers to make it more interesting to reporters. It's got many angles: higher education, finance, women's interest, tech, and the list goes on. The story also goes to local news stations with personal email letters to journalists that might include a catchy subject line like "234 Sugar Babies attend NYU."

Over the next few weeks, I begin to understand exactly how public relations works and what it means to be a PR representative. There's a reason they have a slimy reptation. They're paid to lie. I'm being paid to lie. That's just part of the job description. It's like being a puppeteer, a little bird of sorts. At SeekingArrangement, we're automatically the authority on all things sugar dating. We decide the trends from our data set and convince reporters with a press release and a prayer to cover it. It's the type of advertisement you can't pay for: carefully manufactured clickbait. Better still, readers think it's legit since it's from an outlet they trust, lending credence to our brand.

I was naive to how news is made before working here, assuming new "studies" were all from legitimate sources. Any website or organization can replicate this formula. We design numbers to appeal to certain demographics and interests, angling our pitch to fit whoever we're trying to hook. Since we're the authority, no one asks questions on the legitimacy of our data. How could they? If you don't believe us, then don't publish it.

For big pitches, we make it easy for reporters to build a quick hit. It starts with a saucy press release featuring quippy lines news outlets may want to use for the story, including quotes from The CEO that fit their beat. The second essential part is a press kit. It's a downloadable file with everything they need to accompany their article or segment. Stock photos, infographics, videos, logos, etc. Finally, we seal the deal with not one but *two* sources to interview, both with intimate knowledge of the lifestyle: The CEO and a sugar baby.

Media often can't resist the delicious story, neatly packaged and served on a platter. Perfect for the journalist who's overworked and underpaid. They get an easy byline with great returns; we get free press and notoriety. Everyone goes home happy. It's almost like we're winking at them, and they're winking back – both making a tiny bargain that erodes our souls.

CHAPTER 14

CASTING

"Let's talk about casting," Jackie says. Her Skype pings four times in rapid succession before she taps the mute button on her keyboard, cutting a ping in half.

"Like casting actors?" I swivel around in my chair, our desks opposite each other.

It's been a few weeks since we sent out the sugar baby schools pitch – sugar daddies paying for university degrees – and it's seen some traction. The low-budget video we shot even made local news in Las Vegas. We made a spoof, an infomercial for a sugar daddy. I got a rush seeing the news I helped create on air. *It makes me feel influential.*

"No, case studies for schools. Like, for news segments." Jackie spins around in hers, pulling a few sheets of paper from a binder. "We need to screen the sugar babies and daddies before they can talk to a reporter. And they need to sign our media agreement."

Ah, *casting.* Anthony told me he was the "casting director" when we initially spoke. He made me think I was getting cast on a reality show. Looking back, that title seems like a ploy. Now I'll be the one doing the bait and switch.

"We need to send out a mass email first, to see which sugar babies are interested," she says, opening an email on her laptop to show me.

Paid TV Appearances reads the headline with a short questionnaire and request for a few recent pictures. I remember this format from the email about the reality show casting. It must work, I mean, it worked on me.

"We're going to filter, though," she says.

Jackie sends me a list via Skype, and I understand what she means. It's a list of rules for who will and who won't receive the email. Sugar babies fill out their profiles with demographic information, like age, height, body type, and ethnicity. We use the filter to remove the women Jackie doesn't want to receive the email. Anyone over age thirty, overweight, or Black/African Decent is removed from this listing. I pause. The last one seems racist, but I don't mention it. I'm not trying to ruffle any feathers. *I'm still new here.*

"The girls who go on camera need to be hot," Jackie says, scrolling through the email responses to our blast. Some of the women are half naked, others with rosy face filters. "We want people to see her and *want* to join the site, either to be like her or to date her," she says, still scrolling.

I scratch notes on a pad of lined paper: *must be hot.* My hand is sweaty, the pen sliding through my fingers as I write. Out the window I see thick clouds move across the sky, shading us from the sun and casting a shadow across the block. My temples start to throb. This isn't at all what I expected from my first real job. Lying to journalists, participating in quiet discrimination. I thought corporate America would feel more ... professional. I guess I was wrong.

"Sometimes they can be anonymous, but we can't do that all the time. We need people who are proud sugar babies," Jackie says.

She makes a good point. If we can't get sugar babies who are open about their lifestyle to go on camera, it begs the question: why don't they want to be seen? She passes me a printout with the questions for screening them.

1. How long have you been on SA and why did you join?

2. Have you ever had a sugar daddy? What was that like?

3. Have you ever received money from a sugar daddy?

4. Have you ever had sex with a sugar daddy?

The last one feels like an invasion of privacy, but Jackie elaborates. It's okay if she's had sex with a sugar daddy, but a reporter could get the wrong idea if he gave her money. It's my job to explain and make sure she has a good response. She can't say she's had sex for money, even if she has. It's part of the media agreement.

"We don't want people getting the wrong idea and thinking this is a site for prostitution," Jackie says. "We want to control the narrative."

Has Jackie ever *been* on the site? My own inbox is flooded with messages of men looking to pay for sex every day. So, it's not a site for sex work, it just happens to be full of people wanting to pay for sex. I'm not sure how both can be true, but it's not my job to ask. My job is to cast.

When I manage to get these sugar babies on the phone, most of them have no intention of appearing in the media. They think it's an acting or modeling job, just like I did when I was cast. We're asking them to lie, so it's kind of like acting. I dial the next girl.

"Hi, is this Cassie? This is Brook, I'm a casting director at SeekingArrangement. Is now still a good time to talk?"

"Hi, yeah sure I can talk," a small voice says on the other end.

"Okay great. So, we're looking for people who want to appear in paid media interviews, does that seem like something you'd be interested in?" I ask, feeling like a broken record. This must be my thirtieth call today.

"Well, no, but I'm glad you called. I haven't been able to get through to anyone. I met with a man off the site and ..." She chokes on her words. "And um ... he forced himself on me. He never gave me any money," she sobs.

My chest tightens, breath shallow. This isn't my first time hearing a story like this, and I've only been casting for a week. How many sugar babies do I need to console? Jackie already told me how to respond.

"I'm so sorry that happened. Did you file a police report?" My voice cracks.

"I don't know his real name. That's why I'm trying to contact you," she gulps. "I don't know what to do."

"Okay, I'll forward your information to our customer support department and see if they can help, okay? Again, I'm so sorry that happened."

I know customer support probably won't do anything, but I Skype them her info anyway. Unless we get a subpoena, they won't give out any personal information on the man. Since most people on the site are anonymous, it gets tricky. I hang up and call the next girl.

That evening over bong loads and pizza, I gush about my fancy new job to Jasmin. The shiny MacBook they got me, the video we made that was on TV, and the trip to LA we're planning for a YouTube show project. Jasmin works at a mattress store.

"We're actually looking for a UNLV student to interview for local news, if you want to make some extra cash," I say. I dip my slice of pizza in a Ranch dressing cup and take a bite, assuming she won't bite on my offer.

"Like as a sugar baby?" she asks, tilting her head. Her long brown hair is slightly curled, she brushes it from her face and touches her index finger to her chin.

"Yeah, it's simple, you just answer a few questions on camera about using SA," I say, my mouth half full. "It takes less than an hour."

"I guess I could do it. When, like tomorrow?" She pulls up her work schedule on her phone.

I'm drawn to Jasmin's take-charge attitude, supporting herself and her mother at times. They're from South America; she moved here when she was young. She has endearing innocence but a strong drive that masks her naivety.

"Sure, they can do tomorrow."

I stop myself from saying anything else. I don't want to accidentally talk her out of it and lose the case study. Every sugar baby I find who's willing to go on camera is like a gold star with Jackie and The CEO.

"I just joined though, and I haven't met anyone yet," she says, opening a compact mirror and picking pepperoni from her new porcelain braces.

"Just say that."

The following day, I give Jasmin the spiel – don't say you were paid, don't say you're a hooker, yadda yadda – and she completes the interview with a videographer from a local news affiliate. The turnaround is quick, and the piece airs the same evening. No time for second thoughts. Backlash is almost immediate. Friends, colleagues, and family members berate Jasmin with questions about her financial situation, about her choice to join a website like that. When I get home later that night, her face is buried in her phone. She's wearing her plaid pajamas. The last time I saw her wear them was after a breakup.

"I didn't realize it would air so soon," she says without looking up.

"I'm sorry. I didn't either." I offer my apology, whatever that's worth. I put her check on the coffee table and trail off to my bedroom. I need a shower.

As the hot stream breaks against my back, I get a sensation in my forehead like I'm about to cry. Do I carry blame for this? Was it my responsibility to protect my friend from the inevitable ridicule she would receive as a perceived sex worker? Did I exploit her vulnerability as an immigrant, or just her desire to be on TV? Probably both. I tilt back my head and let the water wash over my face. I feel a few tears join the stream. Deep. Breaths. This is just what corporate America is like … right?

CHAPTER 15

RETURN OF THE TRUST FUND GUY

Oh shit. My internal nag reminds me I forgot to take my birth control pill again. I need to wait until after breakfast or I'll get sick and throw it up anyway but sometimes I forget. It's a whole thing. I pop the little blue pill out of the foil and knock it back with some Sugar-free Rockstar. I went out last night, so I need the extra boost. My phone buzzes at my desk. It's Scott. I look around the bull pen, but no one is here. It's nearly 5:30PM. I answer it. We haven't spoken since he ditched me at Wynn, but he did buy me that bikini, so it wasn't all bad.

"Hey, you," I answer. "I wasn't expecting your call."

"Hey, I'm coming to Vegas this weekend," he says. His baritone voice reminds me of our chemistry in person.

"Fancy that. What are your plans?" I must have made an impression if he's calling me again.

"Just gambling and hanging out with friends. I'm hoping you'll come stay with me," he says.

"Sure. Give me a call when you get to town," I reply.

Stay with him? Like for the whole weekend? I pack a bag and head to meet Scott at the Tower Suites per his request. It's a small red bag on wheels, practical because I'm wearing heels. I find him at check in and he greets me with a side hug as the concierge hands him the black AMEX I remember. I see his name and remember it, just in case.

"Hey, what's all that?" he asks, pointing to my bag and shoving his room keys into the pocket of his jeans.

What's all that? It doesn't even hold very much! He specifically asked me to come down here and stay with him.

"Just a couple things to stay the night," I say, glancing at the floor and turning my shoe inward. I hope he notices my toenails are freshly painted.

"Oh, for sure," he says, oblivious that his very request is the reason I brought this bag in the first place.

I didn't *need* to bring a bag, but I thought he would be expecting it considering *he asked me* to *stay* with him. We head up to the suite. In the elevator he looks down at my bag again.

"So really, what's in the bag?" he asks again, clueless.

"You asked me to stay with you, so I brought an overnight bag." I take the opportunity to remind him.

"Oh, did I?" He's on his phone looking at an email or something.

"Uhm, yeah." I touch his shoulder. "You did when you called a couple days ago. I can just go home later, not a big deal," I say, hoping he miraculously remembers.

"No, stay, it's fine."

I'm just going to leave it. No need to start an argument with a man I barely know, even though he makes me feel insignificant. I certainly won't be overstaying my welcome. We push open the door to the executive suite and I leave my bag in the entry, right next to the door. The living area in this suite is the size of my house, the biggest one I've ever been in. There's cream and gold ornate furniture, marble sculptures, and a massage suite. Two huge bedrooms are positioned on either end of the living room behind double doors. I feel expensive.

"There's a store I want to check out," he says, pouring himself a glass of whisky from the minibar. "It's open 24 hours."

We commission a black SUV and Scott directs the driver to the Adult Superstore. Inside, he starts down the BDSM aisle. "Pick out whatever you want," he says. "I think we should get these," he says, holding a designer bondage kit.

At the checkout with arms full, the total is more than my car payment. The driver takes us back to Wynn, and we get out with our nondescript bags of toys. Back inside the room he wants to try them out. He rips open the kit and starts to tie one of the fasteners around my wrist. I've never been bound, but I'm open to trying it. Before I know it, I'm hog tied on the carpet, a rugburn forming on my collarbone. I'm disgusted, imagining all the gross shit this floor has seen.

"I don't like it, untie me," I say, squirming. My shoulder presses into a brass coffee table leg as I try to get free.

"Wait a minute, let me try something," he says, lifting my skirt and shoving a hand between my legs, pressing me further into the ground.

"Untie me, it hurts!"

"Okay, okay," he laughs.

I make a vodka Red Bull and meet him in the bedroom. We kiss and he takes off my clothes, what's left of them anyway. We have sex for a minute, then he asks me to turn around. Without warning, he pushes himself into my asshole and I scream in pain.

"What the fuck are you doing!?" I recede, a burning sensation takes over.

"Don't be a little bitch."

"We're done here!" I throw up my hands and climb off the bed. "You can go jerk off!"

I grab my clothes and stuff myself into them. I find my bag by the door, right where I left it. Perfect for an easy escape. Are all the men on Seeking-Arrangement lacking decency? Just because he's rich doesn't give him the right to sodomize me without my consent. I didn't even get any money or gifts! What a prick.

Chapter 16

Happy 18th Birthday!
Meet Your New Daddy

"What are you doing later?" a tall, dark, and devilishly handsome man asks me.

He's a model. It's 5:45PM on a Thursday, and the office is buzzing with a photoshoot across from my desk. SeekingArrangement is getting a rebrand, and Jackie says we need new images for the homepage. We're leaning into luxury with a sleek new design. The dated website needs a facelift anyway.

"I'll text you." I hand him my phone with a blank text so he can put his number in. I need to be discreet. I'm at work after all.

"We need to get the *shush*! Don't forget," Jackie says.

"What's the *shush*?" I slink over her where she's supervising the shoot.

"The CEO wants the finger over the lips, like *shush*. It's his jab at Ashley Madison. I told him it's a bad idea." She shakes her head as if to say *boys will be boys*.

One of the many things I've learned in my first months here is about the notorious website, Ashley Madison. It's for cheating and affairs. The founder, Noel Biderman, and The CEO used to be tight, but they had a falling out. Noel created *Ashley Madison*; The CEO made SeekingArrangement. Then Noel launched a direct competitor, Arrangement Finders. They had a billboard last year and got a ton of press.

The CEO hasn't been in the office much. His wife is moving to Manhattan for fashion school. She announced her plans to resign from the office and become a sock designer at a meeting a few weeks ago. I guess that's the sort of thing you get to pursue when your husband is a millionaire. I'm a little jealous.

A few months ago, *Wired* published a story featuring pictures of The CEO holding carrots from my first Seeking photoshoot. The journalist hit the nail on the head: "*The entire marketing strategy for the business is purposefully provocative: from the use of the word "bribery" in the context of dating, through to the frankly astonishing pictures of The CEO dangling actual carrots in front of scantily clad women,"* the article reads. Thankfully, there's no pictures of me.

The strategy works. There are at least two dozen placements every month – long assessments of the kooky founder and his dating websites. Another article reads: *"Let's face it, dating is a very superficial game,"* The *CEO had told the Daily News. "We're simply saying, let's dangle a carrot to get that first date. It's like a pickup line, but more classy and interesting."*

I send a text to the sexy model and get back to my computer. A Day in the Life of a Sugar Baby – our idea for a *Real Housewives*-esque YouTube show – the project on my screen. It's a step in the direction of a reality show, one of The CEO's dream goals. Jackie wants to film on a yacht but pretend that it's owned by a sugar daddy. Brilliant. I peruse through various vessels at the harbor in Long Beach. A faint crackling and spark on set catch my attention. I turn to see a white birthday cake with skinny black candles, Jackie trying to light them with a Bic.

"Whose birthday is it?" I ask her.

"It's for the picture." Jackie smiles like she's got a secret. "For the billboard."

She laughs and places the cake in front of a glowing young woman with her left shoulder exposed. The woman purses her lips over the candles as the camera shutter clicks.

"What billboard?"

"It's going to say, 'Happy 18th Birthday, meet your new daddy!'" She covers her smile with her hand and checks the return screen to see the photos. "Those are perfect."

CHAPTER 17

A DAY IN THE LIFE OF A SUGAR BABY

"We can't use her," Diana says with her hands, holding a retractable pen like a weapon. "Emily got *kicked off Bethenny*!" Diana isn't wrong. Last week she came back from the show in a fit. She's one of the PR managers and scored a segment on the daytime talk show, *Bethenny*, hosted by the *Real Housewives of New York* star, Bethenny Frankel. One of the sugar babies we cast for the piece had a forced exit à la *Jerry Springer*, Diana says. She doesn't want this sugar baby to star in our "A Day in the Life of a Sugar Baby" video.

"Jackie, it was so bad," Diana pleads. "Don't say I didn't warn you!" She throws up her hands and turns down the hall, her heels clicking across the stained concrete.

With every sugar baby I cast, things can go wrong. We need to create original content about our brand, and we need sugar babies to do that. Convincing hot girls to go on camera as a sugar baby in front of their parents and the world is challenging. Half the time they skip out on the reporter, making us look even worse.

Emily, the sugar baby in question, is amazing. She's a well-educated, beautiful, university student. She texts back promptly, and I'm looking forward to meeting her in person. Low key, I'm taking notes each time we talk. "Most sugar babies don't go for the senior citizens," she mentioned during one of our calls. I love her candor. Emily prefers older men, much older. She sets her filter to sixty plus. They're the richest and have a lower sex drive. It's less bang for more bucks, she joked.

I want to understand her. Still on my own sugar journey, I'm hoping to use her tactics to find my own roster of daddies. To me, Emily is living the dream. Her bills are paid, and she spends her nights on luxury dates with interesting men. Granted, most of them are old enough to be her grandfather, but that also arouses my curiosity. How does she sleep with these men? Does she like it? I'm willing to overlook whatever happened on *Bethenny* to find out. Plus, re-casting at this stage would be a pain in the ass. I want to use her.

When Diana is out of ear shot, Jackie turns to me. "She just wants to maintain a certain image. Diana is trying to secure this reality show. Let's see how it goes with Emily, but maybe have a backup."

I opt to drive myself to LA for the shoot. I've been making the drive back and forth from Las Vegas alone since I was fifteen. The wide-open space soothes me. Moving from Southern California left me with the feeling that full green spaces are beautiful. They are, but now I find beauty in the emptiness, too.

On my drive I listen to *Lolita*, the book by infamous author Vladimir Nabokov detailing his innermost desires for romance and intimacy with his prepubescent stepdaughter. I'm doing my research on men. Their peculiarities and proclivities for young, sometimes adolescent, women. Their sweet naivety is intoxicating. A young girl who doesn't yet know the evils around her or the intentions of manipulative men. *A perfect mark, just like I was at that age.*

The following day, I meet Jackie and Emily at the dock for the first part of this shoot. Jackie found a yacht for rent on AirBnB and an actor on Craigslist to play the part of Emily's sugar daddy. It's a perfect seventy-five degrees, and my high waisted skirt moves with the breeze as I make my way through a small park near the parking lot. Not a bad way to spend a Friday afternoon.

"Over here!" Jackie shouts from the bow when she spots me at the edge of the railing. "Don't look down," she says.

I immediately look down and see a dead racoon floating in the water. Jackie laughs. Aboard the ship, I admire the Chantilly lace curtains and the brown on tan with beige accents décor choices. A little outdated for my taste, so I head to the upper deck where Emily and the faux sugar daddy are waiting.

"Emily! So great to finally meet you," I say as she gets up from the leather banquet.

"Brook! Yes, finally." She opens her arms, and I receive a warm embrace. "By the way, I'm so sorry about what happened on *Bethenny*." She touches both my shoulders at once. "They were egging me on backstage, and it looked really bad."

"Please, I'm not upset. If anything, it'll get even more views with a little controversy!" I reach my hand out to the actor, a fifty-something with brown hair and glasses. "Hi, I'm Brook."

The man offers me his hand, limp and … it's *wet*. Ick! His words are inaudible. His eyes are so squinty I can't see his pupils. I shake off my hand

and notice what can only be drool shining on his lip. I'm going to be nice in case he's retarded, but this is gross. Who the hell did Jackie cast? After some failed scene attempts with the man and Emily, Jackie gives him two twenties and tells him he can go. He's a liability.

Back at Emily's apartment in WeHo, we meet with one of her actual sugar daddies for another attempt at filming a scene. Emily has been seeing Bill for about a year. He's sixty-three with a billowing voice and dyed dark hair that still covers most of his head. He's married but agreed to be on camera. He probably controls the finances at home, so he doesn't fear any repercussions for his participation here. What does he have to lose?

I study the interaction between Bill and Emily. How she makes him laugh, how she touches his knee. Emily divulges that Bill usually pays her five-hundred bucks per meeting. Always at her place, always with take-out since she doesn't cook, and they always have sex, which I try not to picture. Is *this* what I want? We wrap the scene and leave them to end the night together.

Chapter 18

My First Party

*B*rainstorm Meeting – Accept? A meeting notification from The CEO slides into the corner of my screen. The description just says to come with your best ideas. It's in a couple weeks. I guess he'll be back in the office. Jackie told me he's usually on some kick after a conference, inspired by whatever was presented on the keynote stage. This time around, he's looking for collaboration and input from his staff. Groundbreaking. I begin a list of some random concepts like a sugar baby calendar; I don't want to show up empty handed. They gave me a promotion, after all, so I don't want to let them down.

It's been nearly five months at SA, but it feels like an eternity. My work speaks for itself. Viral case studies and top tier placements, such as a national segment on a CBS show called *The Insider*. When I cinched that piece, they promoted me from PR Coordinator to PR Manager and bumped my salary up. Anthony was recently let go, so they had an opening. The new title came with a new responsibility: company spokesperson. I was interviewed on *The Insider* as a rep for SA. My fifteen seconds of fame! It ended up being only about five seconds in the final edit, but I felt like a celebrity. *I wonder if anyone I know saw me on TV.*

The brainstorm is the least of my concerns. My first party in New York is in a couple days, and I'm behind on casting. Diana left me a list of sugar babies I need to call. She says they're willing to participate in a documentary, and part of that is being filmed at the party. Diana is working a new show called *This is Life with Lisa Ling*. Apparently Lisa Ling is a high-profile journalist, but I've never heard of her. We need a sugar baby for the show who's willing to be followed at the party and in her life, but it's a big ask for only a grand. I call the first four girls; all have similar responses when they realize it means being on camera as a sugar baby. I call the last girl, a bombshell blonde named Allison.

"This is for a TV show. Like a reality show?" she says. "*Oooh!*"

"It's basically a reality show." I keep the details vague. "We're going to be filming at the party and need a sugar baby to be the star."

"Seriously? That sounds amazing! Sure, I'll totally do it," Allison says. I just hope she shows up.

That evening, I head to the airport for my redeye to NYC. I've been to the city a couple times before with my family, but this is my first time as an adult. Nestled into my window seat, I feel grateful. My first business trip not even six months into my first job. I update my SA profile location to Manhattan before takeoff. Maybe I can catch a daddy while I'm there.

After a shower and a nap at the hotel, I get ready and meet Jackie and Diana in the lobby. The party is in a few hours at Yotel, a rooftop venue in Midtown. It's formal with black and white attire required, as specified on the ticket webpage. I'm so curious to see what sorts of babies and daddies show up.

"Love your dress!" I say to Diana.

She and I are in almost matching floor length, white BCBG gowns, clearly from the same line. I don't love being her twin, I mean we're hardly friends. Diana secured a last-minute placement with *Sky News* with one catch, they want to film right before the party. We're staging a scene with employees that's supposed to pass as a sugar daddy party. Dressed in our best, staff gather at a 30th floor lounge called the Skylark overlooking West 39th Street. The sun is setting and the clouds part to reveal a few last beams. I snap a photo.

"Brook, can we get a shot of you by the window?" Diana requests in her PR voice, several octaves above her regular voice.

I follow her orders like I usually do, this time with a smile because we're in front of Sky News cameras. But also, I'm buzzed. I didn't eat much, and the champagne they served us has hit me.

"And Dave, can we get you next to her," Diana asks.

Dave is one of the devs – short for developers – who code the website. He's a late forty-something white man with a pot belly and a cheesy smile, perfectly representative of the men who grace the pages of SeekingArrangement. *Ah,* I see what's happening. He looks like a sugar daddy, and I'm the sugar baby. We smile and chat awkwardly for the camera.

"Can you put your hand around her waist?" Diana directs.

I cringe. Phil's hand caresses my back and I feel the pads of his fingers through the lace. I swallow forcefully so as not to gag and turn away from the camera. *I hate this.* Thankfully I'm dismissed from my duties as sugar baby on-demand. I arrive to the party at 9:00PM, just as the doors open. Jackie is checking in some guests at the front, so I relieve her.

"Lisa is already here," she tells me, referring to Lisa Ling. "I have to go help her. Are you good here?"

"Totally. I got this," I assure her.

It's a masquerade just like all of our parties. It's the only way sugar daddies will show up. We had an hour-long meeting a few months ago to decide the name of the event – *The Sugar Affair* – but I don't think anyone here cares about the name. Despite the dress code, guests wear whatever they want ranging from floor length quinceañera dresses to men in white button downs and jeans. The ratio is about five babies to every daddy, with most of the women on the dance floor or playing wallflower while waiting to catch a man's attention. Almost everyone is wearing some sort of mask. Ironman, Zorro, and the Phantom of the Opera, among others.

I see guests scurrying up to The CEO to chat. They are forming an impromptu line. Thanking him for his wonderful website, gushing over his latest quote on CNN. He loves it, relishing the attention from his loyal fans. As the event winds down, I maneuver through the women who likely see me as competition, wading through the glances and stares. I want to find Allison, the sugar baby I cast.

There's a side room where Lisa and the film crew are confined adjacent to the dance floor. I find Diana back there being interviewed as a spokesperson. There is a small table filled with flutes of champagne situated beyond various banquets. A head tips back next to the table, and a mess of blonde hair shakes like fluttering leaves. I watch her down half a glass of bubbly. It's Allison, pounding one then another. I try to say hello, but she's whisked away by Diana and the crew for more filming. I grab a glass for myself. After several hours, Lisa and her crew have what they need and pack out. Diana and Jackie are left to deal with Allison who is very inebriated. I see her laying on the banquets, passed out, with her shoes off.

"Is she okay?" I ask while they stand over Allison weighing their options.

"No, she's not. She vomited on my dress and Jimmy Choos," Diana says, wiping her pumps with a paper towel.

The party guests clear around 1:30AM, but Allison doesn't wake up. As I'm cleaning up some odds and ends, I see two paramedics rush out of the elevator. I can't breathe. I won't be the second unresponsive sugar baby at this party. *Oh shit*, is Allison okay? I wait by the elevator until I see them roll her past me on a stretcher, an oxygen mask covering her face. My chest tightens, and I grab my torso. *What did I get her into…*

CHAPTER 19

THE TRUST FUND GUY PART 3: ADVENTURES IN NYC

"What happened with Allison?" I ask Jackie when I find her in the lobby the next morning.

"I had to take her to the hospital, alcohol poisoning," Jackie sighs. "I stayed with her all night, and I put her in an Uber a few minutes ago." She checks her phone to see the status.

The team takes the day to sightsee, and that evening I get a text from Scott. He must have seen me on SA. I give him a call.

"I saw your profile," he says between bites of something crispy. "It says you're in the city."

"Yeah, I am. I'm here for work. Where do you live?" I ask, as if I know the area.

"I'm in Chelsea. Do you want to hang out? I'm about to leave this party, I can swing by and pick you up," he says, and I can hear girls chatting in the background.

"Okay, we can hang out for a bit. I'll text you my address." Jackie gives me her blessing. When he arrives, it's nearly 2AM. He hangs his head out the window.

"Hey sexy," he slurs.

"Oh hey," I climb in the back seat next to him. We share a kiss; his hand finds my breast.

"How have you been?" I realize he's on something, or just drunk, but he doesn't smell like alcohol.

The driver takes us to Scott's building where we're greeted by a doorman. There's gold art-deco metalwork, and the name above the door reads *Walker Tower*. Inside, I'm struck by the air conditioning. It's probably sixty-five degrees. Ten-foot avant-garde canvases on the walls, bronze sculptures of nude women, and get a load of those floor to ceiling windowpanes. I shake off my Vans, and my socks slip on his cowskin rug. I wobble, catching my balance on an ornate coatrack that no doubt cost more than my car.

I'm in awe of the eccentric exorbitance of Scott's life, or the life he wants me to take away as my understanding of who he might be. He must bring so many girls here. What girl wouldn't want to be where I'm standing, or rather sliding, right now? I notice a set of stairs. This isn't even the whole apartment ...

"Who decorated this place?" I ask, admiring the stone fireplace. "It's amazing."

"I did," he tells me, looking me up and down. "I like your jacket. It's hot."

He begins to unzip my black windbreaker. I'm hoping he doesn't notice the hole under the collar, a burn from a joint. Scott must be the richest person I've ever met. Am I *really* here?

"I have some weed if you want to smoke. It's in the drawer over there." He points to the kitchen and takes a seat on a suede sectional.

Every corner is fitted with what appear to be family heirlooms or works of art. Outside the windows, his patio is massive with views of sparkling city lights from atop a golden tower. I open the drawer he pointed to, but there's no weed. Just hundred-dollar bills strewn and a few D batteries. Wrong drawer. I find the jar of weed and take it to the coffee table.

Scott's head is tilted back resting on the sofa, his eyes closed. Somehow, I had pushed the sodomy episode out of my mind until this moment, and regardless of all that, I'm hoping to try having sex with him again. I want the spoils of this life, of what he has to offer. I straddle him and go in for a kiss, but he's not interested. There's something off, like his Xanax just kicked in."

"Are you okay?" I ask seated on his lap, inches from his face.

"I'm sorry, I'm about to pass out. I called you a car. It will be here in a few minutes," he says, struggling through his words. "Here." He reaches into his pocket and pulls out a hundred-dollar bill and hands it to me.

"I wanted something else," I sigh, rejecting the cash.

I put on my shoes. How quickly I went from the girl he wanted to bring home to the one he wants to leave. I take the ride back to my hotel, numb to the disappointment. I should have taken the money. The next morning, Jackie picks up a few copies of the *New York Post*. They ran a story about the party. The energy was not lost on the reporter: "*The pot of gold at the end of their rainbow included a short, balding gentleman with a gourd-shaped nose and two geezers in black suits – one shuffling around in untied orthopedic shoes.*" I read it all while we wait for our ride to the airport.

"Did you have fun last night?" Jackie asks loud enough so the whole van can hear. "Where did you two go?"

"We went to his place at Walker Tower," I say.

"*Walker Tower?*" Jackie echoes. "Isn't that where Gwyneth Paltrow lives?"

"Probably. It was really nice," I say.

From the back row, I gaze out the cab window, enjoying my final moments in the city. As we drive down Broadway toward lower Manhattan, we pass a school donning Scott's family name. I had thought that it looked familiar.

CHAPTER 20

RELATIONSHIPS ON YOUR TERMS

"*SeekingArrangement, Relationships on Your Terms.*" I read the new tagline a few times. It's supposed to signal a different way to date. It's all part of the rebrand, a skin shedding of sorts. All the old verbiage on our website and press releases centered around "arrangements," and now we're not doing that anymore. "Arrangements" are too difficult to explain and justify. "Relationships" are what people find on dating websites. And that's what it is, just a dating site. *Wink, wink.*

The CEO wants to run an ad on Hulu, so we're filming something centered around the "Relationships on Your Terms" theme. The video goes like this: An attractive man walks through a bar; women freeze mid-sip to stare as he goes by. In the style of a video game, he meets a woman, a cute gal in a cardigan. A graphic pops up on the screen: "Stage 5 Clinger." Her inner voice says, "Could he be the one?" Two buttons pop up: "Accept" or "Deny." An arrow cursor hovers over the *Deny* button. *Click*, she disappears. Next, he meets a voluptuous woman wearing a wedding ring. "What my husband doesn't know won't hurt him," she says. *Denied.* The last one is an ethereal beauty with blonde locks. "Hi, I'm happiness," she smiles softly. *Accept.* His final voice over: "Who says money can't buy happiness? SeekingArrangement, Relationships on *Your* Terms."

In my opinion, the video is accurate. SA is all about the sugar daddy. These men fall into categories. There are men like Scott: trust fund, placates women, just wants relationships and sex to be easy, so he pays to keep it simple. The trust fund guy is rare. And as disappointing as our encounters were, I was lucky he's truly rich and that he didn't do anything worse. He easily could have.

There are men like Hector from Mexico, stuck in loveless marriages and looking to be seen as a sexual being rather than the bank account their families reduce them to. Like the great philosopher Charlie Sheen once said, he doesn't pay them to come. He pays them to leave, to leave quietly without destroying holy matrimony. I can't do any more of those, it doesn't align with my main objective: a rich boyfriend. I can't have a married boyfriend!

The other type I run into a lot is known in the sugar world as a "Splenda Daddy." He's sweet, no doubt, but just not rich enough to be sugar daddy. Like the guy who offered to fly me to Tucson for a spa day. He booked me on Southwest and only got me a day pass, no spa services. Splenda isn't going to cut it for me.

Then there are men like John, the first man I met on SA. He uses it as an agency to trick women into sex with false promises. He's not attractive or rich enough to pull young girls, but he knows just what to say to have sugar babies spreading their legs. And he knows right where to look for the most gullible. New sugar baby profiles are easily searchable, so he can see who is likely still naïve. Like I was.

Many of the men are like John. They discover this website, and the clouds open and a light shines on this dark scam where they get to be the man of someone's dreams for as long as it takes to fuck her. The women show up eagerly for their beguilement, falling right into the trap that our marketing laid. Of course, there are bad men who take advantage of the website, many for years on end. Sexual deviants, rapists, con artists. The way SA is designed, everyone is encouraged to be anonymous, to use fake names and burner phones. It's easy to get away with perversions when your identity is intentionally hidden. As long as sugar daddies keep paying, we kept catering to them. *That's* the business model.

The thing all sugar daddies have in common can be described in a single phrase: they're missing something. Be it a conscience, common sense, or intimacy. This isn't limited to just men on SA, it happens everywhere. Maybe they aren't intending to lie, or maybe they're being honest in the moment. Maybe they *really do* want you to meet their friends or take you to Aruba. Or maybe they're just telling you what you want to hear so they get what they want. Usually, it's the second one.

The road to hell is paved with those "good intentions." Men especially like to tell themselves they have the best intentions, always the hero in their own story. They lie to themselves, too. I'm not implying all women are angels, but when they're barely legal they don't have the life experience to see through the *"good intentions"* of a much older man who takes advantage of their innocence, robbing them of it in the process. The shame of being a victim persuades sugar babies to keep quiet when bad things happen. *Especially* when bad things happen. Like when bad things happened to me.

Adding fodder to the flame, sugar babies don't pay to use the site. Most of them are broke and financially unstable. This renders them expendable in terms of our bottom line. The internal logic I gather is that if they don't pay, why would we even consider their wellbeing beyond our technical, legal obligation? Isn't the money they receive enough? Now they want to be protected from abusers, too?

Sugar babies need to make their own mistakes, right? Like I did. How else will they learn? Or maybe … we are at fault for teeing up the ball with our marketing? When I get into these conversations with myself, my belly sinks like I'm falling, and I have to snap myself out of it. I spark up a joint and turn on an episode of *Scandal* to escape the scandal of my job. I can afford cable *and* fantastic weed working here.

CHAPTER 21

LET'S TALK, SUGAR

It's hard to watch, and I don't know why. I need to remind myself to breathe as I scan news segments about SA, one from a St. Louis TV station, another from a Canadian broadcast. I smash the command key, zooming in on my face. *Play again.* I've been giving interviews as a brand spokesperson for a few months, but I hardly feel prepared. The questions are usually the same, but when I listen to my answers, something feels off. Rough around the edges, maybe. I requested more interview prep, and I've been assured I'll have formal media training in a couple months. Hopefully that will help ease the lump in my throat when I watch them back.

Jackie insists I'm doing great. Her protégé, she says. She decided to move her desk out of the bullpen and into a private office since her promotion. She's Director of Marketing now. I get uneasy when she calls me in there, even though I don't think I've done anything wrong. I sit down in the hot seat, per her request. I set my laptop on the edge of her desk and open it, ready to pull whatever information she asks of me.

"Your interviews have been great," she says, always with good news first. "There's something I want you to know." She shifts, pauses. "So you're prepared, in case this ever comes up." Jackie taps a few keys, sending me a link.

I click it open to some article. I scan the words, something about a time and a place, but I'm still lost. "What happened, exactly?"

"The CEO was caught by police in a sting operation trying to meet up with an underage girl," she says. "This is part of why he changed his name. We don't want this story popping up."

"That's ... good to know," I say, not sure how to respond. This is ... *my boss?*

"I'm working on getting this link taken down. We need to throw some money at them."

It's no secret that The CEO prefers younger women – I mean, he's married to one – but this is disturbing. Sure, he got caught once, but it begs the question: What has he gotten away with? The CEO touts himself as a sugar daddy, claims he created SeekingArrangement for men like him. A website designed and curated to protect *men like him*. Ew.

Jackie dismisses me and I head back to my desk, stunned. This is the kind of information that would be terrible if it got out, potentially ending the marketing gambit and becoming the center of conversation. I'm being paid to keep this under wraps, just like any other PR rep protects their brand ... right?

I jump back into the video I was watching, myself on webcam with bad lighting and stringy hair talking about the average age of a sugar baby. Twenty-six, I say. It's actually twenty-three based on the data – which is how old I'll be in November – but Jackie thinks it's better if we say they're older. But I'm different than the other sugar babies. I have a special view, a unique place where I can see two sides of the coin. Both as a sugar baby and from within the platform that facilitates this exchange. I keep circling back to the idea that maybe I can help the other sugar babies with my insight. Maybe some new content, a way to teach them about the pitfalls of the sugar world.

Leaving the office, I'm smacked in the face with smoldering Las Vegas summer air and a bright idea. What if *I* had my own YouTube show? It would give me an excuse to have my own project, and I could get new clothes for it. I feel like I have nothing to wear for these interviews, and I still can't afford anything nice on this salary. But if I was a YouTube star like Jenna Marbles ... things would be better. I wouldn't even need this job. More importantly, the sugar babies on SeekingArrangement need my help. I pitch the idea to Jackie, and she likes it. I name the project *Let's Talk Sugar*.

CHAPTER 22

THE HARBOR HOOKER

As I round the corner from the lobby into the office, I'm met with a few blank stares and a palpable tension. Diana is on her phone and pacing in a red pants suit at the far corner. Her heels tap and tap like a broken metronome. I peer through the interior glass and see Jackie and two of our new PR reps at the table. She waves for me to come in.

"You didn't check your messages yet, did you?"

I have not checked my messages. Last night I went out with another man from SA and stayed up past my bedtime. It shows on my face, which is donning stale makeup from yesterday. I think back to his awkward laugh and his Chicklet-toothed smile. What a waste of time. I ignore my headache and drop my tote on an empty chair, setting my laptop with the others around the table.

"I'm sorry, I didn't get a chance. What happened?"

My chats are filled, it takes me a moment to catch up. Then I see the links: *Call Girl Accused with Death of Google Exec Wrote Facebook Post About 'Killing Sprees,'* one reads. Another says, *Police: High-priced call girl from Georgia killed man, then sipped wine.*

The picture comes into focus as the team prepares the official statement. A tragic accident or possibly a murder took place. The accused and the deceased met on SeekingArrangement. Alix Tichelman met married Google exec, Forrest Hayes, on SA last November. They were hanging out on his yacht in Santa Cruz Harbor where Tichelman injected Hayes with a lethal dose of heroin before leaving him for dead. We're finding out about it now, in July, because the security footage from the boat finally made its way to police and they arrested her. She's being charged with manslaughter, solicitation, and drug counts. Not only that, but she's also allegedly involved in another overdose death in Georgia a few years ago. Not great for press ... or is it? Someone scurries off to post our stuffy response on Facebook, another to take a call with a reporter. Diana is still on the phone with CNN. Jackie and I are the last ones in the room.

"IT just sent me her account. I have the messages," she says.

Her eyes bounce across her screen. I lean in, feeling like we're at the epicenter of a true crime murder mystery with insider access. It's titillating. Alix and Forrest exchanged a few pleasantries before agreeing on a grand for sex. She's clearly a sex worker. "The Harbor Hooker," as coined by reporters.

"This is crazy," Jackie says, showing me the analytics for SA. "I'm glad she's hot."

A huge spike in website visits and sugar daddy sign ups since the story broke. I guess a vixen murderess (manslaughter-ess?) isn't bad for business. SeekingArrangement is where Google executives find prostitutes, so it must be good. It puts us on the map as a "legal" work around to pay for sex. When the site is full of bad actors, a terrible news story is good for business. *Bad = Good. Get it?*

CNN wants to talk to The CEO, but after his questionable responses for the Lisa Ling piece, Jackie is hesitant to have him on the air. He comes off as out of touch and a little kooky, not great for crisis communication. That, and drawing attention to a man who was arrested for attempting to have sex with an underage girl probably isn't the best move at a time like this. Not until they get those articles and his name change sorted.

Diana goes instead. I see her pursed red lips and shoulder pads on the screen and get uncomfortable. She refers to SA as "a beacon of hope" for sugar babies. It's hard to watch, but I can't look away. Deny, deny, deny. The tried-and-true strategy that serves politicians and corporations on their road to power. Bill Clinton's voice, "*I did not have sexual relations with that woman,*" rings in my head. *No, this isn't a website for prostitution. Those users broke our rules. That's against our terms.* Understood?

Somehow the story journalists cling to often misses the mark. Are they or are they not? Is it or is it not? Those questions are a smokescreen for the questions we don't want them asking. How many users report being raped or trafficked or frauded or hurt because of SeekingArrangement? It's a question I also don't want to ask myself.

CHAPTER 23

SUGAR BABY CALENDAR

I saw her suitcase earlier; she always brings it in when she's leaving for a trip. The office is next to the airport off Sunset and Eastern, so she leaves straight from here. When I hear the rolling wheels and click of her heels behind me, I know she's finally leaving.

"Bye, Diana." I raise my hand from my keyboard for a half-hearted *au revoir.*

Off she goes, and the tension in my lungs begins to relax. I take a deep breath and dig into my work. Jackie wants me to take over planning the parties. We're working with a professional event planner this time around, but she wants me to take notes so I can plan the next one on my own.

During the brainstorm with The CEO, he loved my sugar baby calendar idea. The only trouble is now he wants me to make it. Casting a dozen models, full photoshoots, ordering design. I have no idea what the fuck I'm doing. But it feels nice to have projects of my own. I source the wardrobe in my free time and find twelve sugar babies, booking travel as needed. One of them is Christine, my friend and a model who's also a sugar baby. I want a variety of types for the calendar, and she's a bombshell who happens to be mixed race. I'm glad I get to hang out with her for a bit. We don't get to see each other as much now that I'm working 24/7. Plus, I need some advice. My sugar life has stalled to a halt, and this job pays shit. I just wanna have funds.

"I have a question. How do you get any money from these sugar daddies?" I ask her, hoping she's got the secret sauce.

"Go for older guys, or married ones. My favorites are couples. I'm not a lesbian, but I've been one for ten grand!"

Apparently, a very wealthy couple she met on the site came to town last year. They threw her money in chips for her company that weekend and she used it to buy her car in cash. I'm impressed. I wish I didn't have a car payment. Right now, she's driving around a BMW 530i that belongs to some geezer.

"Oh, I don't do anything with him. The car might get repossessed, so he's letting me drive it," she laughs. "I just stop by his place once a week. He's lonely."

Senior citizens and couples aren't ideal, though it is more cut and dry that way. No chance to catch feelings. I want the feelings, though. I want it all.

"I'm dating a photographer. He's like, famous. He took pictures of me," Christine says, showing me some black and white stills on her phone.

I know the guy; I've seen him on the site. He's got galleries here in Vegas at several places. What I don't tell her is another one of the sugar baby models said she's dating the same man. Christine and the other model look similar. I guess he has a type.

The following day, Jackie pulls me into her office. Diana – her furrowed brow in full view – is finger scratching her mousepad.

"We have a situation with one of the models. The red lingerie one," Jackie says.

The hottest one in my opinion. Turns out she had a rough weekend. She stole money and a watch from a man she met on SA. She told him about being cast in the photoshoot and he contacted us to rat her out.

"We can't use her," Diana shoots me a look above her glasses. "She's a thief."

"Oh shit. Okay, I'll let her know," I say.

I don't want to show Diana a reaction. I get the sense she enjoys delivering bad news. The thievery doesn't surprise me. SeekingArrangement has plenty of scammers on both sides of the equation. Put a poor sugar baby in a dimly lit hotel room with a man who won't notice a few hundreds missing from his wallet, and she might make that mistake. I'm just sad it was the hottest one.

CHAPTER 24

CHEAP WHORE

> [Oct 15, 2014 at 8:49 PM]
>
> **Me**: I think we just like to have our own weekends, because we work so much so please let us have that :)
>
> **Jackie**: Yeah I get it, no wonder everyone hates us.. We don't even like each other. I'll keep the weekend free.

Jackie wants to plan a retreat for the PR team, and I'm not sure if she's trying to encourage us to be friends or book herself a free vacation. Her plan is to get us together in a room in Cabo and have us write dozens of pitch letters and scripts. Sounds like captivity to me. I'm setting firmer boundaries with her, like no working on the weekends if we don't have to. Even if it's in Baja, if I'm with her, it's work.

She and some of my other colleagues like to meet up for drinks, karaoke, whatever. Team building, they say. They're close, a few say they're "best friends" having lunch together every day and giggling at inside jokes during meetings. It feels like high school, and I'm not one of the popular girls. My coworkers don't need to be my friends, and I don't need to have a prize-winning attitude to get shit done.

Plus, I'm switching birth control and it's making me crazy. I snapped at Diana yesterday. It's hard to maintain steam when I'm selling a lifestyle I can't afford, moonlighting as a would-be sugar baby. I still can't figure it out. Most of these men are not sugar daddy material, so I'm usually dealing with inconspicuous fakes.

I even have an advantage working here in assessing a true sugar daddy because I can see his profile in admin, the backend of SA. There I can read his messages and find the name and address on his credit card. A little search engine magic, and I'm able to uncover the details on who this man *really* is. Most importantly, see whether he has any reports. If a sugar baby has a bad experience with a daddy, she can file a report against his profile on the website. If he has even one report, it's a bad sign. Still – even with my supposed advantage – I'm not advancing in the "Sugar Bowl," which is what the girls on Tumblr call it. Worse yet, with the new *Let's Talk Sugar* show and brand, I'm supposed to be *giving* advice. Fake it 'til I make it, right?

Last month, I thought I'd secured a decent sugar daddy. We agreed on an allowance of two thousand per month, but he didn't want to meet in public and wanted to come to my apartment. I allowed it because I was desperate for money. He was about three hundred pounds, and I had to drink an entire bottle of wine to sleep with him. Of course, I didn't get the money up front because I'm an idiot. After we had sex, he gave me a mere two hundred.

"This isn't what we talked about," I said, holding the measly bills.

"I'll have more next time," he'd told me. "We'll see each other again this month."

I shut the door behind him and pushed my back against the wall and collapsed. The money floated to the ground. *Two hundred fucking dollars?* After that, I am officially a cheap whore. I'm not meeting up with him again; the thought makes me nauseous. If that's what men on SeekingArrangement are like, then why don't I just become a traditional sex worker? At least my cousin Nancy makes real money.

It feels unfair, but I only have myself to blame. I keep falling for it. What's *wrong* with me? Overworked, underpaid, misled, and left broke on my back. I can't even figure out how to be a proper hooker. And they want me to spend my weekend writing press releases in a hotel room? No. Not for this toxic company. They're so full of shit.

CHAPTER 25

THE BONUS

"They don't want to be associated with us," Diana says between bites of half an avocado, scooping out the flesh with a spoon. "It's bullshit."

"I'm sorry, dude, that sucks," I say. "It will happen eventually."

Diana's dreams of a sugar baby reality show were thwarted once again when her latest attempt at a deal fell through. It sounds like the network had a change of heart, perhaps when they realized the truth about SeekingArrangement and what it does to people. I can't blame them, but I feel for Diana. She's certainly persistent.

My performance review is this afternoon, I keep checking the clock. Finally, Jackie summons me to her office with a ping in my chat. I wipe the sweat off my hands and make my way to her.

"So, what have been some of your biggest accomplishments this year?" she asks.

"Press placements, parties, photoshoots," I say. "There's been a lot!"

"I agree, you're on track to be leading your own team soon," Jackie says, pushing the formal paperwork across her desk. "Do you want to know what your bonus is going to be?"

There on the paper, I see the numbers. Jackie bumped my salary up to fifty grand and gave me a $20,000 bonus. *Twenty thousand dollars.* I stare at the sheet, and it starts to look like another language. For real?

"Wow, that's incredible," I say, trying to contain my disbelief. "Thank you."

"Thank *you!*" she echoes. "Now go get yourself something nice."

She prints me a check because it's too much to direct deposit. This is more money than I've ever had in my life. The drama and annoyances I've dealt with at this company over the last year are in the rearview mirror. All has been forgiven. I can pay off my car, take a trip, do whatever I want. I don't need to sleep with men for money, and I don't need a man at all. It's easy to forget about the morally questionable actions, mismanagement, and turmoil with a fat check in my account. *Cha-ching.*

PART THREE
2015

Age: 23
Playlist: Diplo, Adele, Fetty Wap
TV: *Mr. Robot, Empire, UnREAL*
Favorite pastime: Trying to find a boyfriend

CHAPTER 26

SUGAR BABY UNIVERSITY

Jumpstarting your future begins with choosing the right education. Here at Sugar Baby University, you can gain the personal connections you need to go from entry level to corner office. Enroll with Sugar Baby University today and get your education paid for by a generous sponsor. Because let's be real. Becoming successful starts with who you know. Attending college means you have a choice. Take out loans and eat ramen [womp womp] … or get a sugar daddy and live the life you've always wanted. Sugar Baby University: where beautiful ambitious people graduate debt free.

Jackie loves the script I wrote for the sugar baby schools video this year. I had a stroke of genius with the name "Sugar Baby University," our new branding for this news story about the colleges and universities that sugar babies attend. It sounds like an actual college for sugar babies, but that's just to entice and confuse reporters into taking the bait. Confusion is the strategy that works for politicians, and it works for us, too.

"What do you think of these models?" I show Jackie the roster of girls I've lined up for the video.

I tried to cast something for everyone: a blonde, a brunette, a busty one, and a petite Russian. They'll all be dressed as schoolgirls; one blows a bubble with chewing gum while the other plays with her pigtails. A chalkboard reads, "You+SeekingArrangement = No College Debt."

"Nice. The CEO will like her," Jackie says pointing to the petite one.

"Why? Because she looks twelve?" I joke. I made sure she was eighteen, but she could easily pass for fifteen.

"Pretty much," Jackie laughs, adjusting the oval tag on her silver Return to Tiffany's necklace.

It's like we share a dirty little secret, a sort of privileged traumatic information bond. She keeps me close, her protégé. Last year I threw my first SA party, and it was a bit of a flop. Jackie gave me the responsibility of planning the event but wasn't clear that I was also supposed to be handling the marketing efforts too. When she realized it wasn't being promoted to members, she reprimanded me. How was I supposed to know? I didn't get a list of tasks or anything about a meeting invite. I apologized profusely, but the damage was done, and ticket sales bombed.

"I'm almost done with the numbers," she says, referencing the schools data. "I took the real numbers and multiplied them by four, then added a few to get the ranking right." She gives me a closed-lip smile and turns her screen so I can see the spreadsheet. "We're hitting Texas hard this year."

"Okay, so it's somewhat accurate," I say, scanning the list.

I mean, who can argue? We're the authority. I relish that. As the main spokesperson for the brand, I get to decide what we say to reporters, ergo what the world believes about us. Me at twenty-three years old and Jackie just five years older. We both enjoy the small sense of power it gives us. We're inventing the news here in this tuna can of an office.

When Jackie gets promoted to VP, I'm not surprised. Not because she has qualifications, but because she knows how to manipulate the boss. A gentle song of deference and ass-kissing is an earworm for The CEO. He thinks she's the only one he can trust. Jackie told me he had a bad experience with a former employee overusing credit cards and lying, so he's hypersensitive and controlling of his staff. That's why she keeps us away from him. The new company organization chart has everyone reporting to her or someone under her … except The CEO. She is the only one who reports to him. She says she's protecting us, acting as a buffer so he doesn't force his crazy requests on the team. By my account, she's willing to deal with his antics because the money and status she can coerce is worth it. Sound familiar?

Later that day, I get a call from The CEO. He's livid about a newly released *Toronto Star* article. The sugar daddy for the story is a disaster, even had the reporter to his house for a cringe-worthy photo of him in his hoarder looking bedroom. The article is worse.

"How could you cast this sugar daddy? He's disgusting and not what I want people to think of men on SA!" The CEO scolds.

"I didn't cast him. The sugar daddy I cast is named Stan, that has to be someone else," I say, nervous I might lose my job over this.

It's been a few months, and I don't remember the details. The sugar daddy in the story is named Aaron, a name I don't recall. I call the reporter who assures me Aaron is indeed the sugar daddy I put him in touch with using an alias. *Whoops.* I call The CEO back and lie, telling him the reporter went rogue and cast his own sugar daddy for the piece. Deny, deny, deny. I'm sure that's what The CEO would do if faced with an uncomfortable truth. It's company culture after all.

CHAPTER 27

ONE NIGHT IN RENO

> [Feb 26, 2015, 4:55 PM]
>
> **Me:** This sugar daddy wants to fly me to Reno tomorrow just for like 24 hours
>
> **Christine:** Omg do it!
>
> **Me:** To go or not to go…

Traveling to meet a potential sugar daddy seems like par for the course. But if I were giving advice to a sugar baby, I would tell her: don't give out personal information, book your own travel and hotel, and make sure to get money up front for those things. I don't do any of that.

I've never been to Reno, but he seems promising after I do my requisite sleuthing on his Seeking account. He bought his house in 2012 for nearly half a mil. So, he's got the funds, but a further assessment proves he's married. Most of the men on SA are. I think back to what Christine and Emily told me about how to secure the bag: go for the married guys. They're more generous because they harbor guilt, and they don't take up too much time since they have a wife and kids. I just need to figure out what he wants and whether I can put up with it as a function of how much money he's willing to spend on me. It's a basic cost benefit analysis. James is eager to book me a flight and my own room at a resort. I figure what the hell. He tells me he has two kids, and he's separated from his wife. Code for he wants a divorce but probably doesn't have a prenup.

I arrive on a Saturday afternoon on a Southwest flight. If you ask me, budget airlines have enabled a lot of sugar relationships. Average men can afford cheap flights for their affairs. James picks me up in a Jeep Wrangler, and we head to a local brunch spot. He's tall and tan, Middle Eastern or something with a pot belly in a white button up with French cuffs and silver links. There are worse looking men on SA, that's for sure. At least he smells nice, like Acqua di Gio and fresh laundry.

"If we continue things, I'd want you to get off the site," he tells me over omelets and bacon.

"Well, let's see if we want to continue things. I have some expectations too before I'm closing myself off," I say, pushing the food on my plate around with my fork.

"Okay, I get that. We're going for dinner later at the resort. We should freshen up first."

He pays the bill, and we exit. After all the talk about a resort, I'm shocked when we pull up to a Holiday Inn. "I thought we were going to a resort?" I ask, thinking maybe he's made a mistake.

"Oh, I didn't book you at the resort, this is your hotel. I'll pick you up in a few hours," he says and unlocks the car doors. "Stay here, I'll check you in."

He booked me *at the fucking Holiday Inn!* This man is already getting on my last nerve. What am I even getting out of this? Hopefully he takes me shopping or something tomorrow. He gives me my key card and I wheel my own suitcase to my room in shame, past the front desk attendant who probably thinks he's my dad. James picks me up a few hours later, and we drive to the Grand Sierra Resort where he takes me to a bar all the way in the back.

"I thought we were getting dinner?" I remind him, apparently expecting entirely too much from this man.

"They have food service here," he assures me, pulling out a barstool.

Strike two. We order a bland meal and I drink one too many glasses of wine. He invites me up to his room, and what the fuck else am I supposed do? Go back to the Holiday Inn? We chat for a bit before he decides he's ready for bed. Between the sheets I slip my hand under his boxers and feel the most excessive pubic bush I have ever felt in my life. I gasp in horror and pull away my hand.

"Whoa, you don't shave?" I ask.

"I don't want that tonight."

Thank God. I roll over and fall sleep. The next morning, he takes me to Daughter's Cafe, a restaurant in a cozy Victorian home. From our table in the living room, I have a view of the street through frosted windows. The matriarch cooks a Dutch Baby in a small kitchen, beads of sweat dripping from her temples. It takes forty-five minutes, but the wait is worth it when I take that buttery first bite.

"I'm going to take you to the airport after this," James says from across the table around 11:45AM.

"But my flight isn't until 3PM," I remind him. "Maybe we could go shopping?"

"I can't today," he says. "I'm too tired. We stayed up late."

"I'm just going to be sitting there for hours," I reiterate. "Would you drop your mom or one of your daughters off at the airport this early?"

We sit in silence on the short ride to the airport and share a cold good-bye. *Fucking waste of time.* From his perspective, I should be grateful. He flew me out, bought me food, got me a room. I should be happy, right? The second I show anything less than gratitude with a sugar daddy is the moment it's over. I need to be *appreciative* of a man wasting my time. And never, under any circumstance, should I hold them accountable for bad behavior. They hate that.

CHAPTER 28

SUGAR BABY SUMMIT #1

"He said there's an issue with the unit," Jackie says to our dismay.

We've been waiting to check into this rental since our redeye landed. It's now 1:00PM. Jackie booked an apartment in Hell's Kitchen for the team, but apparently, we're now stranded with nowhere to stay. She finds a cheap hotel last minute and we share rooms instead. We're in town for the first *Sugar Baby Summit,* a conference for sugar babies, followed by one of our parties. I planned both, so this is my moment to shine at the company and in the media. I chose the sessions for the summit based on what I think these sugar babies need, then found people to teach them. The undisputed star of the summit is a stunning sugar baby named Olivia, hosting a master class on allowance negotiation and acting as the main interviewee for several outlets. She's walking away with thousands of dollars from us for her appearances. If they aren't being paid, most sugar babies won't show up. Getting them to buy tickets for this event was nearly impossible, so I started giving the seats away for free. We need butts in chairs for the cameras.

The night before the summit I get a call from *Nightline,* who I secured a placement with. The journalist is pulling the piece because the sugar baby told them she was being paid to appear. *Shit.* The whole story is compromised, and now they can't move forward. Someone on the PR team cast her, not very well apparently. These sugar babies need to be told how to lie.

[Jun 11, 2015, 6:56 PM]

Jackie: Let me know if we can assist in *Nightline.*

Me: I'm talking to the sugar baby when she gets off work, maybe she can call them to apologize and clarify

Jackie: That really sucks. The girls are going to cast in my room when they get back. I'm getting some bottles of wine

Me: I don't know why this happens to us

Jackie: We can fix it. And we have other opportunities if we can't. Did they shoot anything yet?

> **Me:** No they were going to in the morning.... Before they found out we're sugar baby paying deviants. I told the SB who spilled the beans to call the producer and lie her face off

I don't think there's any saving this. Plus, I need to practice my session. I'm giving a talk on "Sugar Safety" tomorrow. It's a lot of common-sense stuff, but I think that's what these girls need. There are countless issues with fraud and scammers on SA. Not only lying and manipulation, but actual financial fraud. If you swap a Nigerian Prince for a sugar daddy, you've got yourself a scam.

I'm almost certain there's no way to stop people getting tricked on the site unless there are some fundamental changes to the mechanics. I might not be able to change the product, but I can do my best to teach sugar babies what to look out for. It's sort of my duty to protect them from what I've gone through. Even if it's a lost cause. I smooth my black pencil skirt, take a deep breath, then pop a couple ibuprofen. I feel a headache coming on.

Sugar babies trickle in when doors open at noon. It's a dimly lit lounge space on the third floor of Stage48, a superclub in Hell's Kitchen with four levels. We hand them a flimsy red swag bag that says SeekingArrangement on the side, so thin it feels like paper. The budget allowed for a branded t-shirt, a red tank top we designed with the phrase "Girls Just Wanna Have Funds" across the front. They take their seats, filling the back ones first to stay out of the views of the camera. Some are wearing sunglasses. Everyone waits for me to step onto the small stage under the low ceilings and bad lighting and introduce myself as the emcee, spokesperson, and reigning queen sugar baby. Okay, not the queen part. But I am openly a sugar baby for reporters. It lends to my credibility. Or lack thereof.

We sequester our media guests away from the sugar babies. We've got the *New York Post, Bustle, Thrillist, New York Daily News*, and the list goes on. Many outlets who've never covered us want a piece of the first ever sugar baby conference. The rules for our journalist friends are simple. Don't take any photos, and don't talk to anyone unless we introduce you to them. Not suspicious at all, right? We say it's to protect our member's privacy.

Two questions from the sugar baby guests rule the day: How do you get sugar daddies to pay you, and what advice do you have for Black sugar babies. We avoid answering both. I can't help but notice that most of the women here are not beauty queens, though there are certainly some standouts. The sugar babies who need the most help aren't the hot ones. The less desirable women are the easiest targets for predators because they have fewer options. They're desperate, and sugar daddies exploit that.

"Do you know how I can buy a ticket to the party?" a homely sugar baby in an oversized sweater asks me.

"We're going to send everyone here a link to buy one. Thank you so much for coming!" I say in my several-octaves-higher PR voice. I learned that from Diana.

Many sugar babies were reluctant to attend the summit for fear of exposure, but the opposite is true of the party since it's a masquerade. Plus, there are daddies there. The trouble we've found is that the women are not always attractive. The CEO is very adamant about the girls being hot; it's part of the brand. We put up a waitlist to create a false sense of scarcity and prevent too many undesirables from purchasing. Then we check their profiles and if they're cute enough, we send them the link to buy a ticket. There are several journalists coming, and we need them to see exactly what we want them to see. But at this point, I'll allow anyone who pays regardless of their looks. We're so underwater on this project, I'm practically a mermaid.

CHAPTER 29

SEEKINGARRANGEMENT PARTY

Perspiration collects on my brow. I dab it with a tissue, careful not to disrupt my makeup. The toilet swirls and there she is again, the girl in the mirror looking more grown up than ever in her red dress and matching lipstick. A few eye drops, an Excedrin in my cotton mouth, and I wash it down with coffee then take a puff of my vape pen. I buy hash cartridges in bulk from a dealer, so I never have to go without weed. I exhale into my reflection, and the smoke rolls across the surface. Do I even like her?

We have just an hour to get ready between the summit and the party which was a horrible oversight on my part. We reserved the third-floor lounge as a hideaway for the press and host our party on the main floor, a nightclub fitted with a mezzanine for VIP and giant disco ball. One by one, even two by two, PR staff lead members of the press into a banquet corral of sorts right there on the party floor. They're allowed to observe, but they have strict instructions not to talk to any guests unless we give them the okay. As for losing *Nightline*, I don't think we can handle any more press, so it's a blessing in disguise that they discovered the ruse. Let's just hope they don't tell the other journalists.

I invited a new POT – sugar baby slang for potential daddy – I recently connected with to the party, and to my surprise he shows up. I offer him a few drink tickets, and we take a lap around the party. I'm in high demand at this event with people pulling me in every direction. New POT is noticeably uncomfortable. I take him up to the VIP and introduce him to The CEO and some other daddies I know. Just then I get a text from Christine, she and a couple of my friends are here. I saved them some swag bags, so I leave New POT and head downstairs to deliver them. When I get back, he's is pissed.

"I'm not going to follow you around like a puppy dog," he says, but all I can think about is his shiny forehead.

"I'm not asking you to, but I need to do my job. I thought you'd be understanding," I reply. "I figured you'd make friends."

"Friends with *these* people? Girls keep hitting on me."

"You're on the site, too," I remind him.

WINK, WINK, NUDGE, NUDGE

"Fuck this, I'm leaving." He smacks his empty glass on the bar.

"Alright, bye." I wave. I'm too fucking tired for this shit, and he's not even handsome.

I find our PR rep, Steven, downstairs working check-in by the door. "How are things going?" I ask.

The flow of guests has slowed, and he alludes to the drama unfolding by widening his eyes and looking to the side. The wind blows a gust of moist air onto my back like she's trying to tell me something. I look up the stairs and see Melissa, another of our PR staff, and Jackie talking by the railing. It looks serious. I accidentally look up Melissa's bell-shaped dress and gasp. Oy vey.

"*I'm* good, but a reporter from Bustle overheard someone on the walkie talking about sugar baby compensation," he says, leaning in. "She's asking questions."

Yikes. We need to keep tighter reins on the media and make sure the narrative stays on track. When the clock strikes twelve, we lose exclusive access to the venue and a swarm of members of the NYU Asian American Club flood the dance floor for their monthly mixer. It's my cue to sneak out unnoticed. I'm starving.

CHAPTER 30

REFLEX MEDIA

I slowly break apart some weed and load it into the glass bowl. It's a new bong I treated myself to after some jerk I went with on a few dates broke my old one. I finally decided to cook for him and that was how he repaid me. Tinder guys are the worst. My new apartment is close enough that I can come home for lunch. I need the break from everyone, but even when I'm not at work, work is all I can think about.

The CEO is buying a new building soon since we're outgrowing the current one. There are several new hires, like an accountant from Arkansas who is also assuming the role of HR. Is that normal? Her name is Margaret, but she goes by Peg, and I feel like the name fits. She's a stout woman who moved here for the job, and I think she brought her son with her because I saw them talking in the parking lot the other day.

We're splitting up the company, and Peg is helping us do it. *Introducing: Reflex Media.* The new sort-of, kind-of, but not really an agency. Or an "incubator" as The CEO calls it. Previously the parent company we worked under was InfoStream Group, which we're keeping, but only for a few people. Everyone else will become an employee of Reflex Media. This is essentially to mitigate legal repercussions. "In case the feds ever crack down on sugar" is the phrase I hear around the office.

I exhale a long breath and sit quietly in a puff of smoke on my narrow balcony. A cloud moves over the sun and the sky turns dark; construction dust blows on the street below. I get a chill, and shudder at the thought of returning to work. The CEO is in today, and he's on another tirade. It seems like every other week he's upset with me, whether it's reprimanding me for something petty or making me write press releases at midnight. Something about a Menendez case? Yesterday I had to pin his lavalier onto his shirt, and it made me sick to touch him. He's never come on to me, but I get the feeling I'm not his type. I hear he has a new girlfriend in addition to his wife, part of his new "ethically non-monogamous" philosophy. I wonder how she feels about that. Does putting a brand on cheating make it okay?

Things would be simpler if I'd gotten that job at the Wynn back when I was eighteen, if only I hadn't failed the drug test. Maybe I'd be a floor manager instead of a stoner. Maybe I wouldn't have to ask myself such hard questions. I load another bowl and try to think about something else. *Buzz buzz.* A text from a random number.

[June 14, 2015, 3:23 PM]

(863) 733-XXXX: Hello this is Sam I am bringing girls down to West Palm Beach to stay at my estate for weekend trips over the summer. Bringing a couple girls per trip paying about 4k to 6k per trip. If you or any of your girl friends are interested please send photos one per message to ensure they are received along with what weekends you are available thank you :)

CHAPTER 31

THE SUGAR MOMMY

I met Katie at Wet Republic pool club one Saturday, and we clicked. She's five-foot three with thick blond hair and eyelash extensions, a smoke show. I'm twenty-three, she's thirty-one, and I think she might even be prettier than me. I mean, her fake tits look amazing. I think she's into me … like romantically. She invited me to dinner at Stack in the Mirage. She insisted on paying, flashing a glitzy Tacori ring, instantly recognizable from the ads I used to see in *Cosmopolitan* magazine.

"Wow, your ring is amazing!" I say as she turns it to catch the light. "Did someone buy it for you?"

Katie looks at it, almost bashful. "No, I bought it for myself. It's easier at work when men think I'm unavailable."

There is a man she's interested in, though. She's going to see him in her hometown of Spokane, Washington, for Fourth of July. "Would you have a threesome with us?" she asks casually.

"Oh sure, that sounds fun!" I half joke, not wanting to deny her. I think I'm into her too.

"Are you serious?" she asks, smiling under her perfectly lined lips. "I'll book you a flight right now."

She takes out her iPhone. Did I just land a sugar mommy? If an attractive man was treating me like this, I'd certainly be game. But I'm not entirely sure about the whole threesome thing. I'd be interested in making out with her, but the thought of seeing her with a man doesn't appeal to me. Then again, I've never been with a woman. What's the worst that could happen?

On the flight, I order a glass of wine and try not to ponder the question. The sticky air in Spokane hits me like a dose of reality, the sun beaming, pavement radiating. Katie rolls up in what can only be described as a hooptie. She hops out and greets me with a warm hug, pressing her firm breasts into mine, her skin moist. She looks different, more of a back country girl with only her eyelash extensions reminiscent of the bombshell I had met for dinner. Without her styled hair and sparkly jewels, I'm not as awestruck. Perhaps the glitz and glam shaded my reality.

"Sorry about the car, this is what I drive while I'm here. I like to blend in."

The sentiment quickly makes sense as we ride past the cheap apartments and overgrown grass. We make a pitstop at a dispensary because she knows I love weed.

"I don't have any cash," I say, having assumed this would be an all-expenses paid situation.

"Oh, okay," Katie grabs a few bills out of her Celine wallet and hands them over.

The tone shifts, and it's not just because I'm high. It feels forced. Maybe she's not the "mommy" I thought. We stop by a liquor store, and she picks out Grey Goose, Bombay Sapphire, and a gold bottle of Ace of Spades Champagne. Or maybe she is …

"I want to get him something nice. He hasn't been home in a while," she says. "He was in prison."

"Are you serious?" I take a shallow breath and hold it.

I spark a joint and ash it out the window as we head through the humble town to pick up the inmate. Former inmate, excuse me. A detail she conveniently left out until now. We pull up to a house with a car parked on the lawn, a common aesthetic around here. A cut Black man in a navy-blue shirt exits the house. As he gets closer, I see the tattoos. Black ink covers his arms and neck. Then I see the ankle monitor. Okay, yeah. He's hot. I let him ride shotgun.

"Man, this is surreal," he says, touching his cornrows and shaking his head in disbelief.

His personality is not what I'd expect from a parolee. Soft spoken, he's grateful for us coming to get him and shy about tonight. Katie tells me they knew each other in high school and started talking again when he got locked up. She booked the three of us a suite at the Quality Inn, apparently the nicest place in the area. Katie's sister is waiting outside the hotel, pacing and smoking a cigarette. A thin woman with long, curly brown hair and a few teeth missing. Katie gives her some money and the car keys.

"Where is she going?" I ask.

"She sells coke, she's getting us some," Katie says, grabbing the felon's ass.

Inside the room, there's a huge hot tub situated in the bedroom that's fresh out of the 80's, complete with wood panel walls and shag carpet. If these walls could talk, I would not want to listen. Katie pops the champagne and pours us a few glasses. Before I can take a sip, she's straddling the felon. What's my role here, the audience? I pour myself a shot of Goose and knock it back, holding back the urge to vomit. Soon the sister returns with the blow and a male guest of her own.

Katie summons me to the bedroom from behind a door at the corner of the living space. I hear the water running and the scent of cotton candy. Katie is hanging off the edge of the tub, nude. She tosses me the biggest box of condoms I've ever seen; it must be from Costco.

"We have to switch every time, so we could end up using a lot!" she giggles, splashing her toes in the sweet-scented bubbles.

Shouldn't this turn me on? I go all the way into the bathroom to collect myself. My hands are shaking, heart racing. I have to go through with it now. What else am I gonna do? Katie wants to watch.

"Kiss him," she says, rubbing herself with a small vibrator as he fucks me. After a few minutes, she's ready for some attention, leading us into the tub.

"Let me see your pussy," she says and squats into the bubbles. I sit on the edge and show her, nervous about what she might think. What if she doesn't like it? Are they very different? I've never seen one in person. "Oh, thank god," she sighs in relief. "Can I?"

"Sure," I agree, feeling the rush of the drugs, my shoulders tense. She's down there for a few seconds, then motions for me to return the favor. I give her a lick before involuntarily grimacing. *Whoops.*

"It's okay," she says, looking down at me with big brown eyes. "I'll just come!"

Without skipping a beat, she squirts on my chest. I'm once again awe-struck. I also want a shower. I dunk into the tub, and the felon gets on top of her. She moans, and I watch, but I don't want to. I excuse myself and do a couple bumps of the cocaine on the bathroom counter. In the living room I find the sister and her guest on the couch, she's riding him and screaming in pleasure. Does that make this … an orgy? This day has been full of surprises. I go back into the bathroom and wait for the couples to finish. When they do, I spark up a joint and blow it out the window, notic-ing the easy roof access.

"I dare you to fuck him on the roof," I say to Katie.

"You dare me?" she smiles, shooting a devilish glare at the felon. Then she does.

Chapter 32

The Lingerie Party

I'm at my desk trying to eat my salad, but there's a sinkhole in my stomach. My dad told me he heard my voice on a radio ad for SeekingArrangement. He said he knew it was me instantly. Our Hulu commercial got pulled for violating *their* terms – ironic since the name of the video was "Relationships on Your Terms" – so we diverted that expense to a Howard Stern radio spot. I lent my voice because I thought it would be fun to go to a recording studio, and it totally was, but I hadn't calculated that my father listens to that very program religiously. I shake out my hands over my keyboard and get back to my email. My GQ placement is coming out soon.

My phone rings, and it's Rhett, a sugar daddy of the past. I met him on the SA sister site, WhatsYourPrice, a site where men pay for dates, a sort of spin off to the classic. It was part of my training to join all the sites and poke around when I started here, and he offered me a few hundred dollars for a first date. I never made him pay me, but he ended up buying me some lingerie and shoes. The sex was always great, but we fizzled. My curiosity is aroused when I see his name on my caller ID.

"I want you to throw a party at my house," he says. "A lingerie party."

I mentioned once that we should throw parties together and he's cashing in on the offer. I am a professional event planner now, so I guess he came to the right girl. "Sure, I can do that."

"There's something else I have to tell you," he says, pausing a little too long. "I met someone on SA. She's living with me."

I almost spit out a kalamata olive. "That's great, I'm glad you found someone."

"She's only eighteen," he says. "She doesn't have a great home life, so I let her move in. At least until graduation."

"Graduation?" I ask, pretending not to know exactly what he means.

"Yeah," he says. "She's in high school."

"I see." I toss my salad in the trash. I'm not hungry.

By the night of the party, I've forgotten about the barely legal paramour. In my full-length mirror, I snap some photos of me dolled up in pink lingerie and sky-high platform pumps. Too risqué for Instagram, but I need a new picture. I haven't posted in a while. Keeping my feed filled with adventure and escapades contributes to my confidence. Likes make me feel liked. I compare myself with other girls, the likes, the locations, even the body parts.

I pull up to the driveway of his Tuscan style home at Lake Las Vegas, ring the bell, and there she is. The high school girlfriend. A ninety-pound girl who reminds me of the petite European I cast for the 'schools' video. She's wearing a red silk robe with an Agent Provocateur set underneath. He only ever bought me Victoria's Secret lingerie.

"Oh hi, you're Brook, right?" She wobbles in her six-inch heels.

They're Louboutin! He got me a pair from Hustler once, but she clearly has him wrapped around her finger. That, or Rhett wants people to see her in them and know he can afford it.

"I am. Are you the new girlfriend?" I force a smile, hoping my face isn't green with envy.

I follow her down the marble steps, across the grand foyer and out to the backyard. It's pitch black beyond Rhett's pool; all I can see is the edge of the water, then an infinite abyss of nothing. I know it's a golf course, but it feels eerie. I find Rhett on a daybed smoking a cigar, wearing just his red silk boxers.

"Brook!" He gets up to greet me. "Thanks again. You rock!" He gives me a thumbs up, then a side hug, and puffs his cigar.

"My pleasure," I say and continue my rounds, avoiding a possible conversation about his new young lady.

A strange energy brews as the eclectic posse arrives. Rhett's friends and their wives, perhaps their mistresses. Some of my girlfriends, two of my coworkers (who I didn't know were fucking each other) and then, *her* friends show up. High schoolers. They're drinking, smoking, and splashing in the pool on a white swan floatie while forty and fifty-something men watch them and practically drool. It feels foul. I go home early.

I bury my face in my pillow that night, smearing the makeup I didn't wash off. I chalk it up to a wild night, another Las Vegas experience. But I can't help but remember the feeling I got when I gave Rhett a side hug. Jealousy. Like I wish he wanted me instead. Don't get me wrong, I could have had him. It didn't work out for a reason, but still,

I had shared intimacy with him. That connection left a piece of him with me and – even though he grosses me out and I have no interest in a relationship with him – I still want him to want to be with me. Why am I like this?

Chapter 33

Reports

[Sep 30,2015, 12:25 PM]

Allison: My POT has a private jet, is popping a bottle of 47k wine on our first date, giving me 5k cash so I trust him up front, and is sitting me down with his lawyer & my ex sugar daddy lawyer to negotiate a contract that entitles me to an automatic payment of 9k per month in an account plus a 5k limit credit card that does not include the cards I will be given to stores he has accounts with for shopping plus a major shopping trip once a month. Like what?! Sugar gold … if we hit it off we leave for Paris for the weekend. Oh, and his dick is broken. So this is fucking platonic.

Me: WTF?!?!

Allison: AND he said if he dies while we are under an arrangement as he is very old and in poor health, I will be paid what I was making every month plus a 5% yearly increase. And every six months my allowance goes up 2k monthly

Me: OMG how old is he?!?

Allison: I'm making him buy me loubies & Louis luggage for Paris. He said he'd redo my wardrobe. And he told me to choose the most exclusive restaurant I want with a waiting list that Beyoncé couldn't get into and he will still make it happen. Any suggestions? I'm gonna challenge him haha

Me: So cool! The French Laundry in Napa is ridic. you have to make a reservation year in advance

Allison: Haha I'm gonna tell him I want it. Oh and when we travel together I get my own prez suite...btw if you're free next weekend and wanna go to Paris he said I could bring someone so I feel safe. No sex no strings!!. I'm gonna feel him out Thursday in NYC and make sure he's not salt 100% but I have a good feelingggg

Me: YES OMGS

Allison: Literally we are leaving Friday night he's gonna helicopter me to his jet or something then jet set to Paris for dinner and shopping for the weekend and then come back so I can teach Monday hahah

Allison: Literally we are leaving Friday night he's gonna helicopter me to his jet or something then jet set to Paris for dinner and shopping for the weekend and then come back so I can teach Monday hahah

 If this is real life he likes to have a couple sugar babies at once so the girls can tan and shop together and they all just hang on his yacht and he literally shuts down Cartier so we can shop like WhaaaaAaaat

Me: OMGGGGGG STOP. I'll quit my job and we can live in a penthouse in the city

Allison: He has a house on the LES with 8 bedrooms. It's 11 mill he said I have access to any of his 6 homes including skiing in aspen

Me: does that even exist lol

Allison: I might be confusing it with his hamptons house lol. But each home is fully staffed with butlers at all times and we have to make lists so they know what kind of bottled water and things must be there for us upon arrival

Me: okay feel him out…

Allison: He has yachts – one is called "diamonds are forever" He said he treats his babies like daughters because he couldn't ever have kids of his own and it kept him from developing a marriage, so now spending his money on us gives him joy and keeps him humble and reminds him that the luxuries are still luxuries. Like how sweet is that?

Me: AWWW

Allison: I'll keep you updated :) the fact that he is down to contract is really a good sign. We ended up on the phone for 4 hrs today. Like we really clicked. I didn't have to fake it.

Me: whhattt that's a good sign

Allison: and he's paying for my lawyer of my choice to review it with me which is very noble and my former sugar daddy who I'm still friends with is a huge NYC lawyer so I chose him! Since he'll understand such an agreement ya know?

Me: thats awesome. You need to get that in writing girl!

Allison: Exactly!!

Me: If you send me a link to his profile I can look him up and see if he's a creep

Allison: He said he's not verified on the site

Me: You don't have to be verified for me to look up his reports, etc

Allison: And he seems like not your average sugar daddy like he doesn't present himself as overly rich because he's retired but idk the way he talks I don't think he's lying

Me: just saying.. better safe than sorry!

Allison: https://www.seekingarrangement.com/member/eXXcXXXX/ Look him upp. Please don't break ma heart

Me: it could be better

Allison: Uh oh what does it say

Me: There's not a lot on him

Allison: Anything bad?

Me: the profile is new

Allison: He was honest and told me he was not verified and hasn't gone through the process – what's a report mean?

Me: Background verification is entirely separate. most men are not background verified, meaning they haven't submitted their social security to be canceled out against violent crimes. a piece of salt with no priors will pass a background check. Reports are member created. So 8 women took the time to create reports on him in the last 2 weeks

Allison: Oh shit

Me: here are the reports
This person had a different screen name, city, no pictures, and now they have blocked me and changed their entire profile. They are trying to scam sugar babies.
Has changed his profile to several different people. 25 year old to now a 42 year old.
Both on 9/28
He is completely fake, writing stories for a paper. 9/20
Sending threatening messages & harassing phone calls. 9/16
His photo is of Colin Wayne. He's not Colin Wayne. 9/16
The fake pics aren't on there anymore. I reversed image searched him and didn't find anything

Allison: He told me about one girl that accused him of being fake so he drove to her in his lambo

Me: That all being said, he could be real still, and wasn't serious about these girls and they're mad.

Allison: Whatever I'll feel it out!

Me: In my expert opinion: This profile was created not very long ago and has gotten quite a few reports. I'm guessing he got kicked off previously with an old account and recently made this one.

Allison: Oy. Well we will see how it goes! It wouldn't be my first taste of salt lol

Me: oh yeah… he has 2 previous accounts

Allison: What??! So lame

Me: this one has 17 reports

Allison: Oh well some things are too good to be true

Me: *"He claimed to be an athlete and 35 located in Miami then a day later totally changed his whole profile and location. He's fishing for girls and taking advantage by lying"*
THIS ONE
This member has been contacting me for a while claiming to be clay Matthews and many other football players. He asked me for money and is trying to scam women on this site claiming to be a football player and asking for help claiming he will then fly me or others out to Green Bay and watch him play.

Allison: Hahahahahahaha

Me: this seems to be the common consensus: *When I spoke to him last week he had a completely different profile. As in a entirely different person. Income. Profession. FACE. Two completely different men.*

Keep him in your back pocket.. but at least you know. if you ever want me to look someone up I can. I hate to be the bearer of bad news but I'd hate more for you to get fucked over and waste your time

Allison: So true! Ugh all this salt makes me thirsty

Me: yeah and he's messaging some other girl that looks like you as we speak. he has a thing for blonds. he says this to every girl:
Id love to discuss a sb contract with you. Emails & texting is for fakes. Id want to call you once then arrange a face to face anyplace youd like have a friend present to make you feel safe I fully understand. Id even be willing to fly you private anyplace youd like for some fun shopping for yourself and a friend on our first meeting. There is a major status difference between a real sd and a wanna be.

Allison: Omg

Me: and he calls them all and talks to them

Allison: I feel like guys who mention the fakes and wannabes are usually the fakes and wannabes … real rich men are too focused on their money to be focused on other men #realtalk

Me: AMEN

CHAPTER 34

THE DOCTORS

It's a perfect seventy-five degrees –the day before Halloween – as I drive down Melrose, the Hollywood sign playing peekaboo between the streets in the distance. The sun is shining, and my aspirations are playing out in real time. I drive slow with the window down so I can take it all in. I pull up to the gate of Paramount Studios and take a breath and a beat to fully appreciate the moment. The guard takes my ID, and I look up at the grand stone arch, the one I've seen in so many shows and movies. The security guard hands me a printout with an Admit One ticket at the top and a map to my destination at the bottom.

Diana is pitching the *Let's Talk Sugar* brand to anyone who will bite. My tagline is "The Ultimate Sugar Baby Guide." It's a blog website with various posts and a YouTube show, but I have plans for more. This appearance is a step in the right direction. Producers and journalists are not just nibbling but sinking their teeth into this female-centered spin on sugar. It's in line with new wave feminism, or so we say. *Let's Talk Sugar* empowers sugar babies. They're able to take control of their dating lives and ask for what they deserve. That's our story, and we're sticking to it!

Daily Mail, New York Post, Cosmo, and more, all want a piece. But the one I'm most excited about is a talk show on CBS called *The Doctors.* I follow my map to Stage 30 as golf carts zip by me down the alleyways. I try to catch a glimpse of who that might be. A producer meets me outside the metal double doors and walks me up to a private green room. I'm early. I wanted to make sure to arrive before the sugar babies. I can't have them alone with producers.

I check myself in the mirror, my pink BCBG dress, rolling my shoulders back and practicing my reactions. Recently I started getting lip injections and I'm still trying to figure out how to smile. Then I see it. The August issue of *GQ Magazine.*

Inside is the first magazine print piece I've placed; it's finally come out after over a year of back and forth. Taffy, the journalist, got together with my favorite case studies, Allison and Emily. She met with them in person but offers anonymity with aliases like Kitten Babypuss and Tigress St.

Fawn, respectively. I skim through the glossy pages, my hands moist with sweat, and find the article titled, "How Sugar Daddies Make it Happen." It's one of the best articles I've read on the topic. The author is candid and broaches topics with levity and understanding. She writes:

> That, my friends, is the scam, here at the intersection of greed and loneliness and insecurity and the basic human need for survival. You can tell yourself whatever story you want, and eventually you'll forget you're telling a story, and you'll find yourself in the parking lot of a Pizzeria Uno getting sucked off by someone who thinks she's getting the better end of the deal. And the worst part is, you'll think you're helping her. And she'll give you that blow job, all the while wondering how she could get so lucky, how you could be so dumb. Everyone gets what they want. And, sure, what's so wrong with that?

Absolute poetry. Though it hits different after I spoke to Allison the other day. I'm planning to see her in December for some press in NYC, and we caught up over the phone. I like to keep my case studies in my back pocket, check in now and again. She told me she lost her job teaching dance after *This is Life with Lisa Ling* aired. A few parents had a moral quandary, and she got the boot. That didn't surprise me. What did surprise me, though, was her perception of Lisa. Allison said she tried to back out from the project after thinking about it further, but Lisa convinced her. Told her it was important to tell her story and alluded to helping her with a book or involving her in other projects. Allison regrets doing the show, a common sentiment among sugar babies who participate on camera.

In walks Maria, a gorgeous single mom sugar baby who I cast for the show. Her perfume fills the room, her bronzer sparkles under the vanity bulbs. She's followed by a second sugar baby, a young student. Both are attractive, as per our requirements. They've just been shuffled through the halls by a producer and seem frazzled.

"Hey ladies! How are you?" I ask, rhetorically of course.

I know neither of them want to be here. The two-grand payout is too good to pass up. They exchange a nervous glance with each other, both hoping the other says something first.

"I'm okay," the student says, brushing her hair behind her ear. She looks down at her phone. "Is there a penalty for leaving?" she asks, her voice quivering.

"Oh, I don't know, didn't the casting director talk to you about that?"

I know the answer, but it's better to play dumb with these girls. I won't mention the media agreement they signed, a scare tactic that states if they fail to appear they could be liable for damages. I can't have her leave, that would look terrible and might become the storyline on air. Why would this girl back out at the last minute?

"Okay, I'm just getting really anxious," she says with a furrowed brow, nearly in tears.

"You don't need to say anything," I tell her, softly closing the door. I touch her shoulder gently, "I'll do all the talking. Promise."

Then a knock at the door, a producer. "Alright, we're one minute out, are you ladies ready?"

"Yep, we're ready," I say through the door. "Trust me. It will be fun," I tell the sugar babies, looking them each in the eye for a moment before we're paraded onto set.

I hear the crowd snicker and groan as I'm introduced. They're just jealous. Not everyone gets to be a guest on a talk show. The interview is quick – about three minutes long – and as promised, I do most of the talking. The single mother sugar baby provides one response, but I take control of the line of questioning. What's so wrong with wanting a rich boyfriend? Is it a crime to have standards? *I didn't think so.*

Chapter 35

Airline Hustle with
The CEO

The CEO told me he'd meet me at the airport and give me my boarding pass there. I'm flying to New York for a couple projects. When I arrive for my flight, I'm confused as to what the hell is going on. Is The CEO coming with me? Why can't he give me my boarding pass in a text message or email? Must be something to do with his airline status because he flies so much. He meets me near the baggage drop and takes my suitcase.

"Here's your boarding pass, use this one to get through security," he says, handing me the slip. "I have to check your bag, wait here." He rolls it to the counter.

I'm still confused, so I wait patiently and try not to look rattled. He finishes quickly since we're the only ones there.

"Once you get through security, let me know and I'll send you the first-class boarding pass for your flight," he says.

"Have you done this before?" I ask, a little concerned.

"Yes, it will be fine. Just let me know when you're through security," he says.

It takes me a minute to understand what's going on. The CEO bought me one ticket that I'm using to get through security. Because you can cancel within 24 hours for a full refund, he'll wait until I get past, then call the airline and say I had to leave for an emergency, canceling that flight.

By that time, I'm already at the gate for the other flight he booked … under *his name*. Once I'm through, I text him. He sends me a QR code boarding pass with his name on it. He gets upgraded for free, but only if it's *him* who's flying. That's where the swindle comes in. I use the boarding pass that says his name, which bears no gender stereotypes, an essential detail for this to work.

"Thank you, Miss CEO," the desk agent says, which makes my back stiffen and my stomach turn. I head down the jet bridge and wonder if this is a crime. It seems I ask myself that a lot at this job.

CHAPTER 36

THE REFLEX PARTY

"*Confessions of a sugar baby, I got $500 for sex with a 75-year-old grandpa – but I'm not a hooker,*" reads the front page of *Page Six* next to a picture of Emily looking expensive in a red dress and lip.

Emily lives in the city now for school, and I met up with her my last night in New York and introduced her to Allison. They are two opposite ends of the sugar spectrum. Emily is quiet, reserved, and doesn't wear much makeup. She's not on the prowl per se, but probably makes more money than Allison and girls like her. I mean, Emily is willing to date grandfathers and quadriplegics for a few hundred dollars, which she likely squirrels away. Allison wants Louboutins. Not the same.

I'm glad I got to connect with them both, but I fear the fallout from this story could leave Emily in a similar position as Allison, ostracized and unable to pursue her professional goals. I guess we're all in the same boat. Regardless, it's always nice to see a huge story go to print, and today I'll really get to soak up the accolades. Tonight is our company holiday party.

This week, both SeekingArrangement PR coordinators quit, and I can't blame them. They hated working under Diana, and unlike me, didn't have an exit plan to get out from under her thumb. The team also hosted a volunteer event at a local organization for homeless youth. The CEO didn't attend the event but snuck in at the end with a Reflex Media shirt for the group photo, since legally he can't be within a thousand feet of centers for children.

Jackie and Peg organized the party, but those two and Diana are on my shit list after writing me up for some bullshit. A bad interview in *Bustle*, a bad press release, I'm all bad, bad, bad. Two years here seems like a lifetime with the tensions and the turnover. I suck it up for tonight. I must show my face. Bonuses are coming.

Arriving at the venue, I'm struck by a full-on 50s diner themed house replete with checkered floors and red patent leather booths. *Where the fuck am I?* Just then, I notice someone who looks like Tara, a sugar baby I cast for the calendar. I do a double take. That *is* Tara from the calendar, a tiny thing wearing a faux fur vest and skinny jeans that show off her tooth-pick legs. She's only nineteen and I'm not sure what she's doing here, I thought she lived on the east coast.

"Is that Tara?" I ask Jackie.

"Yeah, The CEO invited her," she says, pointing at the two of them chatting in the corner. "I think Tara and The CEO are … an item."

"I see," I respond, attempting to hide my disgust with minimal words.

Did I put her on his radar? I say hello to Tara but keep the conversation brief. I don't want to get involved. About thirty minutes later, another sugar baby The CEO invited shows up and drama ensues. Tara gets drunk and starts crying about the other girl, and Jackie is on damage control. I don't have the energy to deal with this, so I disappear into the karaoke lounge. Most of the staff is hanging out there to see employee performances by Backstreet Boys and Journey.

In a corner booth, I notice Peg's freckled face. She's sitting stiffly with her hands in her lap like she's never been to a party before. When she moves, her tight strawberry blond curls stay firmly in place. Next to her is the young guy I saw her talking to outside the office. He's short and looks about eighteen. Her son, I think. Then I notice he's tickling her back gingerly and I'm instantly nauseated. I guess that's how they do things in Arkansas.

PART FOUR
2016

Age 24
Playlist: The Weeknd, Cashmere Cat, Justin Martin
TV: *Westworld, Animal Kingdom, House of Cards*
Favorite pastime: Pool clubs and dog things

CHAPTER 37

THE SUGAR BOWL

Leaning back in my desk chair, I scroll through the comments section of my Instagram page for *Let's Talk Sugar*. Memes like a picture of Kim K crying in bed with the caption, *"When you thought he was real, but he turns out to be a piece of salt,"* cover the feed, my own handywork. My brand is supposed to be relatable yet specific with a splash of levity. The sugar babies are eating it up. My eyes dart around the engagement on my page. It is intoxicating. I read a few comments. One asks how to know whether a sugar daddy is a scammer. *Delete.* Another says the website is just full of "salt daddies," the name coined for fake men on SA. *Delete.* Jackie told me to remove the negative comments, so journalists don't see them. Here's one I can answer: What's a Diamond sugar daddy? "These daddies pay more to be featured and have their incomes verified!" I write my response. *Send.* It's true that we let sugar daddies pay a premium to be featured on the homepage. At one point I think customer support verified their income with a tax return, but that stopped with volume. Now we just say we verify their income. I switch to the forum on the *Let's Talk Sugar* blog. The questions there are more interesting.

Even before SA, the sugar community was exceedingly online. Yet they live a lifestyle that values secrecy and capitalizes on shame, making the internet the perfect, and sometimes the only, outlet for babies and daddies. However, not all sugar babies are happy with the new attention. SA has seen the bubblegum-ifacation of sugar. Since I started working here, sugar culture has seen a shift. It's supposed to be a lifestyle of discretion, but the marketing is contrary to that fundamental aspect. Colloquially called "The Sugar Bowl," some sugar babies have been in the scene for years, long enough to see a rapid decline in the quality of men. Even Christine and Shayla told me they don't use SA anymore because there are too many fakes.

SeekingArrangement used to be more fringe. The most common way someone would learn about the site was through word of mouth, making it an exclusive club for like-minded people. Rich married guys would tell their rich married friends about this sneaky site where they discreetly pay for sex from hot, young college girls. The best part? The girls aren't pros and will accept much less than a traditional sex worker, and they don't have the perceived stank of a weathered whore.

It wasn't so bad when less people knew about it. More hush-hush as opposed to a national phenomenon. I helped to change that, for better or worse, but mostly just for worse. Especially after the Alix Tichelman story of the Google exec who was murdered on his yacht, the site has become an attractive place for unsavory individuals. There are horrific stories all the time where people met on SA went on to victimize their date. But it's not just men who are the predators, like the *New York Post* story titled *"Twins held in robbery of 85-year-old sugar daddy,"* among many others. When the stories that come out are bad, it attracts bad actors on both sides of the equation. They look at the sensationalized story and think, *hey, there's a website out there where people are doing this or that. And look, here it is in the New York Post, so it must be legit. Maybe I can bait my next mark on Seeking.* The ultimate wink, wink for predators.

Indeed, they can. And they do. There is a huge problem on the site with people defrauding sugar babies through common internet schemes like the Nigerian Prince email scam. It goes like this: a sugar daddy sends a sugar baby a message saying he wants to send her some amount of money before they've even met. These girls range from gullible to desperate and often agree to the transaction. And before she knows what happened, he will send her, say, $2,000 and ask her to send $500 back for whatever bullshit reason. It's a fraudulent check. She doesn't know this, gets the check and subsequently sends the money. The sugar daddy's check bounces. She's out $500.

But the latest scam, pillaging through sugar baby funds, is more terrifying. A scammer reels a sugar baby in, promising her an upfront allowance. *Score*, she thinks. I got me one! Then, the scammer asks the sugar baby for her banking details and create a fake screenshot to show that they sent money to her account. The sugar baby doesn't receive anything and informs the scammer it didn't go through. He insists that he did send the money and coerces the sugar baby into sending her username and password so he can check for her. She falls for it.

Most sugar babies aren't old enough to be familiar with these schemes and don't have the life experience to understand if something sounds too good to be true, chances are it is. The shame of being fooled keeps them from coming forward. It's easier to just forget it ever happened than to admit they fell for such an obvious ruse. I try not to think about the time

Kris scammed me or how I was robbed of my dignity by the liars. I was relatively lucky.

The waters have been muddied, and there's no going back. It's led to the seasoned sugar babies clapping back on social media and sending us hateful emails about how our marketing leads to fake people using the site. Interestingly, this creates more competition in a world that used to be so exclusive. The site once had a lot more *real* sugar daddies. Now it's just the salt and Splenda with the true daddies almost impossible to find. Instead of improving the site and protecting members, we focus on strengthening our public image. I might not be able to tell the girls directly that Seeking-Arrangement is not what it seems, so instead I write a sugar-coated blog for them to read.

> *Scoring an arrangement complete with an allowance is no easy task. There are only about fifty percent of Sugar Daddies willing to provide monthly allowances. Most of them are looking to pay bills or help with college and provide nice things, but a monthly stipend is some next level Sugaring.*

We always capitalize "Sugar Baby" and "Sugar Daddy" because we want to indicate respect for the titles. My overarching idea with the brand is to unite sugar babies so they can exchange stories and tips, relieving some of the isolation that comes from sex work. Though we don't advertise it this way, being a sugar baby is certainly a form of sex work and often involves much more emotional labor than a prostitution relationship. *Let's Talk Sugar* is a home for propaganda that will hopefully help sugar babies to redefine this gray area as a romantic relationship and stay legally absolved in the process.

CHAPTER 38

JET SET SUGAR

"Stay sweet!" I hear my own recorded voice say.

My *Let's Talk Sugar* YouTube show is in production and I'm reviewing one of the videos, my fifth time watching it. "Stay sweet" is the signoff line I came up with, paired with a wink and a smile. A reminder to be nice to these men or you won't get a dime. I take a screenshot and post it on Instagram as a teaser, scrolling my feed. Sugar baby social media includes pictures of money and gifts from sugar daddies. Most of them don't like me reposting their pictures on *Let's Talk Sugar*. Some even call me out by name, creating their own nasty posts about me. I guess if I have haters, I've made it.

Successful sugar babies aren't usually flaunting it online. If they do, they keep their identities hidden by not revealing their faces and using pseudonyms. There's one sugar baby I've been following for a long time who goes by *Jetsetsugar*. Trips to Bora Bora and the Maldives, galivanting around the south of France, and a half dozen Chanel bags. She posts her stacks of cash and shows off the house her sugar daddy bought her. She fascinates me. I message her on Instagram, and to my surprise, she messages back. She says she's going to be in Vegas soon and is willing to meet up. I'm thrilled, but not just for the social media clout. I want to study her. What is she doing to get ten grand per month from not one, but two sugar daddies?

I meet at Lavo with Monica and her friend, Lillian, for brunch. They're staying at the Venetian, so I suggested this place after she turned down my initial suggestion of Sushi Samba. Monica hates sushi. When I arrive, they're already seated. I order some mimosas for the table. Monica is studying the menu, shaking her head.

"I'm picky, everything they have has nuts or sauce," she says, running her long, manicured finger across the page.

"They can make it to order or get something from next door if you don't see anything," I say, carefully observing her response.

"Can I get plain buttermilk pancakes and syrup on the side? Just plain, no toppings," Monica asks the waitress, twiddling a gold Micheal Kors watch on her thin wrist.

We cheer with our mimosas and Monica snaps a picture for her Insta-gram. She posts it right away and tags my *Let's Talk Sugar* page, which I wasn't expecting. Hopefully she isn't the next recipient of hate comments.

"My main sugar daddy begged me not to come this weekend. He of-fered me an extra five grand to stay home, but I said no. I needed to get out of town," Monica says. "He's like, obsessed with me."

I'm utterly captivated. Monica is mixed race with chocolate skin and long black hair with straight across bangs. She confesses it's a wig and uses a small comb to align her bangs to perfection every so often. She's easily six feet tall and slim with large breasts. She's wearing black ballet flats and a simple pink dress. She's beautiful, of course. But there's got to be more to her game. I ask leading questions and lean in.

"What are your sugar daddies like?"

"Old, rich and married," she laughs, and her perfect white smile beams. "Beverly Hills is crawling with them."

Her success has amounted to tens of thousands in the bank, a house, an investment property, and a trove of handbags. She supports her family and is taking a European vacation this summer with them. That's what motivates her, long-term wealth and taking care of them. Monica has two sugar daddies, one gives her ten grand per month, the other seven grand. Neither knows about the other and she makes them feel like they're the only one. She sees them each about once a week. One likes to meet at the Beverly Hills Hotel and the other at her place. There's sex, but the emo-tional labor is more taxing, she tells me in not so many words.

"Ugh, he's texting me now. He thinks I'm partying with guys here, so he gets nervous. He's controlling," she says, typing a message back to him.

Monica makes them feel special. She boosts their egos without requir-ing them to form a deep connection. Most women want the connection, and then they're open to intimacy. Sugar babies offer intimacy without the need for connection. And that's what these men love. For Monica, I think they fetishize her. A drop dead gorgeous, voluptuous Black woman with endless time and no requisite for commitment is likely the opposite of their wives.

It didn't start out at ten grand per month, she tells me. She's been see-ing one of them for years, the other for just over a year. At first it was just five hundred per meeting, until he asked for exclusivity. Then she asked for more, and slowly upped the ante as her living situation changed. She doesn't care about the Chanel bags and shoes; she wants money in the bank. The trips are just a bonus, and it works for her. She must be the exact caricature of perfection during her vacations, and that costs extra.

"I don't live the Beverly Hills lifestyle like most of these sugar babies," she explains. "I'm discreet. That's why I don't post my face. I like to stay under the radar."

Her remarkable fortune can be attributed to a perfect storm of factors. Proximity is the main one. Without being local to LA, she wouldn't have met these men on SA or been able to continue the affairs. Her looks are undeniable, but it's the time that she's invested that sets her apart. She doesn't have a job. Sugar daddies are her job, and she takes them seriously.

A few weeks later, I notice that Monica deactivated her Instagram. I ask her about it, hoping it's not because I reposted her pictures. She had nearly eighty thousand followers.

[April 18, 2016, 10:59 AM]

Me: Hey girl! Just want to see what's good with you! I saw you deactivated your account and I hope it's not cause I posted

Monica: No girl! I don't mind being posted. I just deleted my sugar instagram because I have two really good sugar daddies and I don't trust the girls on there, so I deleted it.

Me: Okay good for you! They don't deserve you anyway

A week later, I post one of the pictures we took together not showing our faces. I get a message from Monica the next day.

[April 29, 2016, 3:23 PM]

Monica: Hey babe. Do you mind deleting this pic from letstalksugar? All the money shots can stay. I had a horrible incident because someone recognized my necklace, purse and bikini. People are so nosey

Me: No prob! I'm so sorry about that

Monica: It's not your fault at all! It's just pathetic people with nothing better to do.

Being affiliated with Seeking is essentially asking to get burned. Sugar babies online hate us, and they especially hate me. That's the final piece, discretion. Monica isn't out there flaunting it. She doesn't care for the social media clout and keeps her circle tight. Her life is quiet, enabling her to be with married men. All factors considered, it's becoming clear that I'm never going to prosper in sugar like her. I want more. I want it all.

CHAPTER 39

SUGAR BABY SUMMIT #2

"There's a lot riding on this. Someone was fired last year for how she acted at the party," Diana says, as though she's passing down the lore of SeekingArrangement.

Seated around a dining table at our rental off Beachwood Drive in Hollywood, Diana gives them advice that feels more like a threat. She hired two new PR coordinators to work under her after the last two quit. From my assessment, these two also don't like her. I don't think they like me either since I made them share a room. The house is just a three-minute commute to our venue, The Avalon Hollywood, which is a nightclub now, but was originally a theater. It's been around since the 20s, and the optics speak for themselves. VIP booths cascade up in the back of the auditorium, gold railings that pop against burgundy carpet. We're using the banquets as a media section, per usual, a playpen of sorts for our esteemed guests.

The morning of the summit, I saunter into the ballroom which is wrapped in paneled LED screens on a backdrop of long curtains. The juxtaposition of old and new is exactly what I want guests to feel, symbolic of sugar relationships. Our *Sugar Baby Summit* branding scrolls across the screens. It feels major. This time around, I'm not leading a session. It was too much last year. I got more qualified speakers and paid them more this time around but haven't seen the final products for their talks. I should have been more specific in their contracts; I couldn't get any of them to rehearse with me. My thought is that they don't want to make fools of themselves, so they'll have something solid prepared.

My strategy half works. Some sugar babies say cringey things, like Fatima, a six-foot tall, curvy Instagram influencer who is clearly not prepared at all. Or my Brown Sugar Expert who didn't know that the term "brown sugar" refers to the community of Black sugar babies. But the worst was probably Ava who, when asked how much money she gets from sugar daddies, suggested sugar babies check local escort prices to know how much to charge.

All the press attendees want to interview The CEO. It makes him feel important. If we can keep him occupied and make it look like there's a lot of media attention, he's happy. It's hard to quantify the efficacy of public relations, though some analytics of sign-ups can be traced to web hits. But brand awareness and impressions aren't measurable in a data-specific way. We certainly aren't making our money back on ticket sales. It's more of a vanity project for The CEO. A way for us to maintain the constant flow of media coverage that he so desperately desires. The party is tomorrow, another song and dance where he's the most important person in the room. Dealing with The CEO is like theater. Fitting, since we're in one. It's exhausting.

CHAPTER 40

AP

I've truly become friends with Allison, the sugar baby from *This is Life with Lisa Ling*, and it's heartbreaking to learn she can't keep a job. Part of me is like, well, she should have thought of that before she agreed to do press. The other part of me says, yeah but, *I convinced her*. I told her she'd be a reality star. I let her get guilt tripped by Lisa Ling. I tricked her with the promise of stardom, like Anthony tricked me years ago.

There's a tipping point for the sugar baby case studies, so we rinse and repeat, both for them and for us. Eventually the cost outweighs the benefits for them, and they no longer want the association. By that time, it's too late to save their reputations. Allison's entire livelihood is fractured and maybe beyond repair because of a clickbait story people will forget about in a few weeks. That's the thing about digital media: it lives forever. Replicable in perpetuity. We used her, then hung her out to dry. She chased the dangling carrot of fame and was hit with the stick of losing her job and winding up strapped for cash. Now she needs us.

At a certain level of faux fame, we can't use case studies anymore because if we repeat the same ones too many times, it becomes tired. No one wants her anymore, and it signals that maybe we keep using the same girls because not many are willing to come forward. And maybe, *just maybe*, things are a lot worse than they seem. Fresh casting attracts new journalists and keeps the cogs in motion. I exhaust sugar baby case studies while I can. Then I ask them to make up a new story for anonymous interviews. Most of them don't want to be themselves anymore anyway.

[May 29, 2016, 11:51 AM]

Isabelle: Hey! The AP article is finally up

Me: Yay! I would read it.. But I don't want to deal with work right now lol. Maybe you can read it and tell me how it is

Isabelle: They picked the worst photo of me lol, but the article is ok

Me: Omg no it's so pretty!!

Isabelle: My eye looks weird lol

Me: Shut up you look like a goddess

Isabelle: Aw thanks. When u get a chance when you're at work will u put in the payment for the article, thank you!

Me: Yes we will transfer payment on Tuesday

Isabelle is a busty law student who was a speaker at the last summit. Smart, beautiful – and somehow willing to go on the record as a sugar baby – she attracted the interest of the Associated Press and, to my surprise, was willing to do a story for them.

[May 29, 2016, 7:40 PM]

Isabelle: Omg the story got broadcasted by so many news stations

Me: Yasss the plan worked

Isabelle: It's on daily mail, abc san diego, msn, philly inquirer, cleveland, detroit. So many haters on facebook. Crazy!!

Me: Damn!! That is nuts

Isabelle: I know omg people are hardcore hating on me in the comments lol

---

She sends me five screenshots of the various articles, probably hoping we'll pay her more. I don't think she knew who AP was, and I was banking on that naivety to convince her to participate for a measly five hundred dollars. The AP certainly didn't know we paid her. The story made headlines across more than a dozen major metros. This one piece got as much attention as the entire summit. Good for me, terrible for Isabelle. I think that bridge is close to being burned.

[May 31, 2016, 5:04 PM]

Isabelle: Hey question about the pr job ... what's going on with that? I may not be taking the bar anymore

Me: Oh no! I forwarded your resume to Diana, she does our hiring. you can email her to follow up. why aren't you taking it anymore?

Isabelle: Lol after AP no way any firm is gonna hire me

Me: I doubt that, and you can always use another name

Isabelle: I don't even wanna study it started last wk i haven't done shit lol

Me: haha! yeah, law isn't easy

Again, the tug of war. Is it my fault? Hers? Neither? Both? Questions I don't have the desire to ask. Instead, I insist she should work for us to butter her up, the highest level of flattery I give sugar babies. First reality star, then employee. Don't worry about your future employer seeing this, *just work here.* With me! xoxo. Plus, Isabelle doesn't want to be a lawyer. She wants to be a sugar baby. This exposure could help her reach that goal instead. Isabelle tells me she's going to be in Las Vegas this weekend, and I feel obligated to meet up with her. It's the least I can do.

I meet Isabelle in the line for Harrah's buffet. She's a Persian bombshell with a valley of cleavage in a floor length maxi dress. We chit chat, but eventually she breaks down. She's going through a total crisis, just got a tattoo, and is reconsidering her entire schooling journey. It's not that she blames me, but there is a certain sob story element. As though maybe I can do something to help her. What I offer her is more ego boosting and convincing her she doesn't want to be a boring lawyer. But a man will respect that she understands litigation. Then I take her out to the beach club for some day drinking. Getting sugar babies drunk is always part of my game plan. Tell them how hot they are, buy them a drink. I put a cherry on top and tell Isabelle she should move to Vegas, and I'll hire her as a PR coordinator. I'm sure she'd be amazing at it, but the next day I come to my senses. If I want to help Isabelle, she can't work here. She needs to get far away from SA. But first, I need her to do an interview.

[Jun 6, 2016, 10:54 AM]

Me: What are you up to today? just heading to the airport?

Isabelle: Ya prob just hanging around here then airport

-[continue]-

Me: Dopeee. Do you want to interview with British GQ? $300 for name only, $500 if they use pics

Isabelle: Sure pics are fine. I'm supposed to do australia sometime this wk too!

Me: Thanks! Also.. I was thinking about you this morning, and I don't want you to make any hasty decisions during your mid life crisis. Like of course I want you to move here cause that would be fun.. but the job you'd have would be tedious, and you might not like it. You'd be hired on a trial period, which means if things didn't work out, you'd be sort of stuck. And I wouldn't want that to impact our friendship. Basically.. I think you'll be better off meeting your whale benefactor as a part time lawyer than as a PR coordinator. You can take the bar next year or something too, or even in Vegas. I get that you don't want to work.. like who does.. but the guy you want will respect you and be more willing to accommodate you if you do, or at least fake it.

Isabelle: Yeahh i get that thankss ill thimk about it. I think the job would be fun though the way Diana described it.. I still have to figure out what I'm doing about the bar though

Me: Sure it's fun, but it would be a lot of blog writing and casting at first. Which are not the most fun tasks. I did that basically non stop for 1.5 years

Isabelle: thats the LA guy if u get a chance look him up

She sends me a sugar daddy profile link. I don't think she liked my attempted heart to heart. It's for her own good. Again, it's the least I can do to look this man up in admin for her. She mentioned he was a creep.

Me: No reports on him.. weird! He probably makes new accounts when they get suspended

Isabelle: I also don't think he used it that much bc he had the girlfriend for a while. But that's weird

Me: yeah a lot of guys have several accounts, especially the ones who fuck girls over.

Isabelle: Ew

The cycle of abuse comes full circle when Jackie dangles the same carrot in front of me that I did for Allison and Isabelle.

[Aug 10, 2016, 5:34 PM]

Jackie: Just took a call with a production company. They're interested in the summit and you (leader of the sugar babies) As a reality show concept

Me: Love that! The Secret Lives of Sugar Babies

Jackie: As well as a rough outline of our plans for world domination with our sugar baby army. It's still very early talks, but the guy used to work on the Kardashians

Me: Yeah sure, what kind of articles, just good placements or LTS articles?

Jackie: Anything you think makes for a positive or interesting portrayal of the sugar baby summit movement. Also keep it on the dl, I'm doing this with The CEO not Diana

Me: Gotcha. Yeah sure

A part of me holds hope, but that hope erodes with every broken promise. I still want a reality show, but now it's just to plot my escape from this place. The CEO, Jackie, and Diana would be forced to respect me. If I'm the star, I'll hold the power.

Chapter 41

Back on My Bullshit

I really want to go to a cooking class, but all the good ones are for couples. I settle for a Knife Skills class instead. At least I'll get out of the house today. My dating life is a revolving door. If they're on SA, they lack the ability to form a deep emotional connection, or they have their wife for that. Sugar daddies want women to be easy, and I'm not an easy person. I play insincere all day at work, I just want to be real with my partner.

PrinceCharm messages me on the site, a profile with no picture and a brief bio. He wants to meet for dinner. I do my usual digging and see that he's been on SA for a year with no reports. A further dive reveals he owns a lucrative company. And better yet, he's cute. He's not going to be on any magazine covers, but the good-looking ones usually like to show off. Relationship Status: Separated. I am curious what sort of code he's sending with that. Salary: $1-10mil per year, and he might be telling the truth.

I meet Yousef for drinks at Vesper Bar inside the Cosmopolitan. I used to meet guys here before I was twenty-one because I could sit down without being carded. He's shorter than I imagined but matches my energy perfectly. We talk about podcasts, and I make him laugh with my dry sense of humor. He gets shy when I ask about his relationship status.

"We've been separated for about a month; we have a son in elementary school," he tells me. "But I love coming to Vegas, and I needed it this time."

Usually having a kid would disqualify him as a potential suitor, but there's something disarming about him I find endearing. That, and he laughs at my jokes. We spend a couple hours at the blackjack table where he loses at least two grand but doesn't bat an eye. I always like it when a man can lose without a reaction. If he didn't have it to lose, he shouldn't have played it. I'm the real prize anyway, and I'm going back to his room with him.

Our chemistry is amazing, and the sex feels natural. He's a sultry lover and takes his time, spending hours in tantra until dawn. I wake up to room service and a forehead kiss, and we both pretend we didn't just meet a few hours ago. I never like to stay too late the next morning, so I gather my things and head out.

"Do you want to come to TAO beach today? My friend and his girls are going to be there," Yousef asks.

"Sure, hit me up," I reply and make my departure.

I always leave the ball in their court. If he really likes me, he can do the work of texting me. I'm thankful when he does, just a few hours later, requesting my presence at the beach club. He says the girls want to go shopping later, too. I hope the other females don't pose any problems for me. I know how catty women can be, especially when resources are at risk. Lucky for me, the girls are drunk and seem to be only interested in Yousef's counterpart who flew them out from Minnesota. This is the first time either of them has been to Las Vegas. I don't ask how he knows them.

"We want Neverfulls from Louis!" The blonde one squeals.

They're both adamant about going shopping, specifically for monogram bags from Louis Vuitton. At least they have goals and aspirations. After polishing off a bottle of Grey Goose, the five of us head to Crystals mall, home to a row of all the luxury brands: Hermes, Dior, and of course, Louis Vuitton. Yousef and I veer in the opposite direction of the trio.

"Can I buy you a dress for tonight?" he asks.

"Yeah maybe, let's see if I find anything," I reply with manufactured indifference.

He offers to get me a bag, but I feel yucky about it knowing the other girls are using his friend for a purse as we speak. I don't want Yousef to think I'm using him. Not yet anyway. Outside the Louis store, Yousef and I peer in from the walkway and see his friend paying for the purses which are being wrapped in tissue. He shoots us a look and shrugs like a simp.

"What a sucker," Yousef says.

I laugh, and we both pretend we're better than that. We actually like each other. *Right?* The next day, I get a Venmo from Yousef for fifteen hundred dollars with "Versace Versace" as the note. My heart flutters, could this be *a real sugar daddy*? I didn't even have to ask. We keep in touch and make plans to see each other again. He's going to London for a wedding, but he wants to see me, after he returns, in Miami for some big college football game. A few weeks later, Yousef sends me another five hundred so I can buy something cute for our next rendezvous. He asks if there's anything else I want, so I suggest a hotel in Seattle for my upcoming trip to visit a friend. He books me a corner suite for three nights, nearly two grand. He's spent a small fortune on me in just two weeks.

Now *this* is a sugar daddy. It's the closest I've ever been to the life I'm faking. Maybe I'll find success on SA after all. The push and pull of the sugar daddy pursuit is dangerous. It feels like swimming in a rip current. I try to paddle back to shore, back to my sensibilities, but the mystique of the high life at my fingertips sucks me out into open water. Sharks circling smell my blood, ready to shred if I let my guard down. The harder I fight to get away, the stronger the force keeping me here becomes.

Chapter 42

London

An involuntary smile is plastered on my face as I board my first transatlantic flight. I'm hosting a sugar baby coaching event for *Let's Talk Sugar* in London, and The CEO booked me in business class. I recline the seat into a bed, just like I've seen in the movies. It feels like I'm scratching the surface of stardom. I resist taking Instagram photos and just soak it in. The sparkling wine greeting, the zippered bag with an eye mask and socks, and the tiny cup of warm nuts. This is the luxury a sugar baby should experience. And I didn't need to sell my body, just my soul.

I tell Lucy from *The Times of London* to meet me an hour after the sugar babies arrive so I can buy them drinks and meet those who've been cast in person. Two sugar babies are being paid, and they're willing to appear in a photo for the piece, but of course they're late. Sugar babies always want to talk sugar when they get together. For most, this is a secret from their friends and family. They find a sort of refuge at my events.

We're gathering in a muggy basement bar, one of the only places that would respond to me when I told them I was hosting an event for sugar babies. Next time, I won't be so specific. Surrounded by taxidermized birds and cave-like pink walls, I'm sweating. The girls arrive and naturally form a circle around me, their host, but I don't say much. I want to save my breath for when the journalist gets here.

"I was recently scammed out of six thousand pounds," says a thick woman with an Australian accent.

I cover my mouth and gasp, though I'm anything but shocked. She better not repeat that in front of the reporter. "Oh, my." I clutch my pearls. "What happened?" It's good to understand the issues.

"He told me I was going to be his assistant. He sent me a check and told me to buy a computer and mail it to him, then the check bounced." Her eyes glaze over.

"That's terrible." I cut her off, hoping to circumvent the waterworks. "I'm so sorry that happened. Why don't you send me an email with his info, and I'll take care of it." I lie. "Do you want me to review your profile?"

A variety of young women, and eventually a male sugar baby arrive, about twenty in total, far more than I expected. I tell them about the journalist who will be here from the *Times*. I anticipate they'll be hesitant or reluctant, but to my surprise many are willing to talk … for free. Uncoached. I hadn't expected such an eager bunch. The prosecco must be working. Lucy, the reporter, arrives and she's swarmed by sugar babies before I can run interference. I attempt to get my talking points in.

"If women want to be escorts, there are plenty of other sites for that," I tell her. "This is a dating site."

"How much does your sugar daddy give you?" Lucy asks, pen and notebook ready to strike.

"I'm not going to tell you, because that would be totally inappropriate," I reply, tugging at her innate desire for British etiquette. I furrow my brow to hammer it home. "I will tell you he's in his 30's, and we really enjoy each other's company."

I don't share too many details. I'm supposed to be meeting him at the end of my trip and I don't want to jinx it. I give her my best celebrity-keeping-their-relationship-under-wraps energy, but I'm the least interesting one here. She chats with some of the sugar babies, and I want to follow her but that would make it seem like I need to babysit, or maybe I have something to hide. There are some attractive girls, one of whom is clearly a sex worker. Donna is an eighteen-year-old from Manchester with platinum blonde hair wearing ice blue contacts and a white miniskirt. She's not shy about her conquests. Her sugar daddy owns her flat in Chelsea where she lives with her friend. They get their rent paid in exchange for threesomes and sex on demand when he's occasionally in town. She's heading to a sex party in Sweden next week.

As Donna speaks of her escapades, my hands ball into fists. How could she be so blatant about prostitution in a place like London where they value privacy? I'm mortified but know the sick truth. The worse the story, the better for business. The crasser and more abhorrent, the better. When it's filled with divisiveness, it gets more clicks, and more pervy men make profiles. That's the PR strategy at work. I hear some of the sugar babies hooting and laughing, and I inch closer to listen.

"How old was your oldest?" one of them pokes.

"Sometimes it's best not to know," another replies. The others chime in, sixty, fifty-four.

"Sixty-four!" says the one who posed the question, a tall slim Black woman with braces. "My sixty-four-year-old sugar daddy was the best thing that ever happened to me." She tells us how he brought her out of poverty, helped her get back on her feet after a challenging year of setbacks. "My sugar daddy turned me into a butterfly," she says.

It reminds me of Diana's quote on CNN a few years ago about the site being a beacon of hope. I guess even a broken clock is right twice a day. I notice Lucy sitting in the corner with a sugar baby who looks like she's about to cry. All I can do is keep the prosecco flowing and throw back a few glasses myself. When the night winds down and the sugar babies leave, Lucy approaches me again like a student who's just completed her homework. She tells me some of the girls had encounters with creepy and possibly dangerous men, that several of the attendees were straight up prostitutes.

"There are people who are trying to screw you over and manipulate you at every corner of your life," I say, dabbing the sweat off my hairline with a cocktail napkin. "It's not our job to police who's an escort and who's not. My goal is to cultivate a community that promotes sugaring."

I give her the best answer I can muster and pay the tab. I've had enough questions for the night. Plus, Yousef is in town and we're meeting up later. I wonder who he's here with. Probably his wife.

CHAPTER 43

MIAMI

[Wednesday, Oct 5, 2016, 7:24 AM]

Jackie: Hey.. Been watching the news. Do you think we should cancel and have you fly back before it hits Miami? Hurricane is supposed to hit tomorrow night and could impact all weekend.

Me: I'm thinking we might have to cancel.. I'll wait until tonight to send out a cancellation email. I don't mind just hanging out.. I'm supposed to meet up with a friend this weekend

Jackie: But where are you staying? You might end up getting evacuated

Me: Staying at one hotel for two nights and then switching to another for the weekend

Jackie: Ok you won't be able to get out after tomorrow and won't know if it's really bad until it's too late.

Me: Thanks! I'll do some more research and let you know!

Jackie: Entire state of Florida is under state of emergency lol

Me: okay thanks. Fatima says it will just be some rain

Jackie: Lol. Does she have ESPN?

Me: Among other skills

I might have to cancel my event, but there's no way I'm cancelling my trip. A sugar daddy once told me he goes down to his villa in Cabo and has watch parties when hurricanes hit. That's more my style. Rich people know what rules to follow and which ones to break. Picture this: Yousef and I stuck in a tenth-floor suite at the Fontainebleau ordering room service, making love, and online shopping for days on end because nothing is open due to a tropical storm. There's no way I'm missing this. Jackie doesn't know who I'm staying with, but I could tell she was prying. I used to share my life with her, but now I hardly tell her anything. I know she repeats things to The CEO and my coworkers, and I'm done being a scapegoat and topic of conversation.

Arriving in Miami it's balmy, a little windy with vaguely gray skies. *Hurricane, shmurricane.* I meet Fatima at my pop-up venue, a private area in her friend's swanky waterfront restaurant in South Beach. When I arrive, she's standing in the dining room on the phone with the owner.

"Okay thanks, babe. I'll let her know," she sighs, flipping her blonde hair over her shoulder, revealing the tracks extensions. "Well fuck. I guess they're closing tomorrow."

Fatima is a six-foot-tall curvy influencer with a big personality. She's Indian and Brazilian and was previously married, as arranged by her family. I follow her flip-flop clad feet for a few blocks until we hit Fifth Street where we find a modern Italian restaurant and grab a seat at the bar. She orders from the bartender in English, then switches tones and languages when she realizes he speaks Portuguese. He's flattered by whatever she says and offers us free drinks. Full of surprises, she is a model, actress, and dancer who uses every element at her disposal to get what she wants. And she has expensive taste.

"I'm living at this guy's vacation rental. You should come by, it's beautiful." She sips a glass of Pinot Grigio.

"What about the hurricane?"

"Oh yeah," she says, pushing her gnocchi across the shallow dish. "So annoying."

The next day, I'm due to check into a balcony suite at Fontainebleau with Yousef. Light rain taps outside and dark clouds swirl overhead. When Yousef arrives, it's like we never left each other. I love his humor and his willingness to hear my facts and stories. Yousef and his friend are University of Miami alum, and the football game we came for is a ritual for them. Riding through Miami in a custom Mercedes-Benz Sprinter that resembles a beige leather spaceship makes me feel like royalty.

After the game, Yousef and I go to LIV Nightclub with a few of his friends. He seems to know a lot of people here, double kissing cocktail waitresses, pointing and nodding at random patrons. I invite Fatima, who shows up with another sugar baby, Veronica. Veronica is a fit Brazilian who wants to talk my ear off about tips for finding a man on SA, asking if I know anyone. She needs to find someone before her visa expires. She doesn't want to settle for just anyone; he needs to be wealthy. Looks aren't as important to her. I tell her I'll let her know. Fatima gets cozy with one of Yousef's friends.

She turns to me and says, "I can always tell when guys like feet." She points her thumb at Yousef's friend and shakes it. "He's been looking at mine." She wiggles her piggies at the edge of her white, kitten heel sandals.

143

The following morning Yousef and I have a cuddle in bed, enjoying the last moments together before we check out. I don't want to leave this afternoon before asking him: *What are we?* It's a conversation no sugar daddy wants to have, but we can't be having this sex and these experiences without feelings being involved … *right?*

"Do you think I'll ever be your girlfriend?" I ask him, resting my head on his chest.

"Yeah, I do," he says without hesitation.

"Like, when?"

"Maybe in like, three months," he replies with an inflection that almost sounds like a question.

"Okay," I say. "I hope so." I like the answer, so I choose to believe him. "Is there anything that would stop us from being together?"

"No. Nothing," he says and sounds certain. "Let's go to the Apple store. I'll buy you the new iPhone."

Leaving him is hard, but the new phone eases my pain ever so slightly. I'm almost twenty-five now. I need to start thinking long term. Being with Yousef makes me think I might have a shot at happiness and maybe a way out of this job.

Chapter 44

Spiraling

I look down to check my phone again, but still nothing. It's been six days with no texts or calls from Yousef. I figured after sharing such a perfect weekend and the girlfriend talk, he'd at least have the decency to text me back. On the seventh day he finally texts me … *We need to talk.* I already know it's bad, but at least he responded. Being ignored is so much worse to me. A non-answer is the one answer I can't live with. He calls me on FaceTime, and I scurry to my car parked outside the office.

"Hey, uh, I'm sorry I haven't talked to you this week. I had a lot on my mind," he says through sighs.

"It's okay. What's up?"

"I don't know how to tell you this," he says, taking a big inhale before his next sentence, though I'm already certain I don't want to hear it. "But, uh, I got my wife pregnant and I'm having another kid."

A lump is stuck in my throat, and I can't breathe. I try to hold back the tears, but looking at his face sends one down my cheek. I force an audible gulp. I could be with a man who has a son and an ex-wife, but he said *wife*. And she's *pregnant*. That's very different. The reality that we can never be together hits me like a Mack truck.

"Oh," is the only response I can muster. I'm suspended in time, my brain short circuiting as I look for words. I return to my body and manage to say, "Congrats." I sound empty, like in the interviews I give. Soulless, manufactured, and insincere.

"Thanks, she's due in February."

"Oh wow," I say, defeated and heartbroken.

Just when I began practicing what I preach. I finally met a man who spent like he was the real deal. There I was at the pinnacle of my sugaring, now falling far from grace. When I get home, I take a long shower and cry. Of course it wouldn't work out. Of course this man was placating me. Why would he need to pay a girl if he were a good guy? *Am I that fucking stupid?* Just as stupid as all the other sugar babies, clearly.

I curl into a tight ball on my couch, dry heaving and bawling. My little dog licks a tear from my face. I had decided to get a dog at the beginning of the year, hoping to help with the depression and loneliness I suffer from this job. Men don't want to date me, daddies are all full of shit, and the isolation is wearing on me. I pet this furry white belly and bury my face in his coat. He's the only one who's there for me.

When I return to my desk the following day, I learn that the founder of Backpage was arrested on felony sex trafficking charges. It's not the sort of news we take lightly around here. There has always been an air of guilt at the company where they throw around the phrase, "if the feds crack down on sugar" to describe the imminent war we are forever preparing to fight. The enemy combatant might be closing in on our ally, and it's time to keep our ears to the ground. In other words, The CEO is spiraling.

Backpage is a website that facilitates sex work, and subsequently sex trafficking, with its interface. I first became familiar with the site when I was fifteen and was shown my cousin's escort ad. It's widely known as a hotbed for illegal activity, but until now has been allowed to exist in the shadows on a legal technicality. With these allegations against its founder, the legality of SeekingArrangement and sites like it are exceedingly compromised. The CEO could be next, and he knows it. His paranoia is at an all-time high. Jackie is concerned about reporters coming to us with questions. I study up. It's best to be prepared for the worst.

Both SeekingArrangement and Backpage occupy the same gray area in the eyes of the law. There's a US code, Section 230, that protects websites, stating that they aren't legally responsible for content their users post. Like if someone is committing slander and talking mad hateful shit on Twitter, Jack Dorsey can't be sued. It makes sense, but also allows dating websites to be absolved of liability when bad things happen. How could a website be liable? That's where the gray starts to shade people's judgment. How far can a website go before they're partially to blame for the crimes of their users? To be determined.

CHAPTER 45

CAUGHT IN THE ACT

"Hey Brook," Diana says, swiveling around in a rolling chair as Peg cocks her head to eavesdrop. "I need a favor."

Diana clicks her pen a few times. I'm sure I don't have time, but she and I have somewhat of a truce these days. I'm sharing an office with Peg until we move into the new building. Last weekend we all went to Peg's wedding at one of those cheesy chapels downtown. I was relieved to learn that the young man from the holiday party was her fiancé, not her son.

"Would you be okay with going back to London for another pop-up?" Diana smiles, her dimples showing. "It's for Channel 5."

"How could I say no?" I reply. "When do you want to do it?"

"Next week," she says, which for a second I think is a joke. She's serious. "Alright. Do you have a venue?"

"Well, I also need your help there. I'll do all the casting if you can book it and get me the budget." She turns to Peg, "Which is where I need your help." Diana flashes a smile that means we all need to stop everything and do what *she* wants us to do.

"I know just the place at the sister property of where I want to do the summit."

I'm thinking of the Haymarket Hotel's French-feeling private board-room. It's in their basement adjacent to a dreamy indoor pool with pink lights. I wanted to use this space for a party, but I can't stand the smell of chlorine.

This is behavior typical of Diana, requiring resources at the drop of a hat. *Startup culture*, they call it. Ready to pivot. Resourcefulness and adaptability. Thrives in a fast-paced environment. Basically, must be willing to work late and get up early to get your own work done because you need to accommodate whoever has the biggest problem. At least this time I get to go back to London and enjoy some delicious duck liver pâté.

To get a huge news outlet like this, there are layers of lies. First is the baseline lie, that Brook of *Let's Talk Sugar* fame is touring the world, hosting sugar baby coaching sessions, and she's coming to a city near you. Get your popcorn and your funnel cake because this is a spectacle your viewers won't want to miss! If Diana can get them with the hook, she swoops in with the second lie: Brook will already be in town. *No, no, no,* she's not flying for ten hours on the condition that this story happens, she'll already be there with real live sugar babies who will appear on camera. Then the most important lie: These sugar babies are certainly not being paid. Just ask them. They'll tell you. They simply love the lifestyle and feel the need to share their stories. They only want to date rich men. Is that a crime? Let's break the stigma! Feminism! Empowerment! See you then, x

Diana and I arrive in London the following week after landing at three connections. Working with her has been smooth as of late. I'm an equal, and she's been forced to treat me as such. I'm the hook. She doesn't have to like me. She *needs* me. The one skill Diana lacks is deference to authority. She thinks *she* should be VP. I know Diana is on thin ice in a power struggle with Jackie, but I don't mention it.

Diana and I meet the sugar babies at the venue around 5:00PM, an hour ahead of production. We need to coach them in person before the journalist gets here. You know, put the fear of god in them, just a little. We discuss a sort of good cop-bad cop situation. I'm their friend, a fellow sugar baby who wants to teach them the tricks of the trade. Diana is my strict and stuffy PR manager with a perpetual resting bitch face. Don't mind her, *this is gonna be fun!* But don't say anything bad about the site, don't say you're a hooker, and don't say we're paying you each a thousand pounds. Half up front in cash, and half via PayPal after the piece airs. *Ready, go!*

All the sugar babies are in uni (which is what they call university here), and one is an American studying abroad. They're a bunch of gems. The interviews are fantastic. The reporter hits a couple tough questions but goes easy on them. I think he likes the American. The girls deliver smart answers and take to my coaching and prep like true Sugar Baby University scholars. I couldn't have said it better myself. Once everyone is shuffled out, Diana and I trade satisfactory glances before going out to dinner to celebrate our win. We find ourselves in a romantic Italian place at a small table on the patio. Diana orders a bottle of Pinot Noir. After a glass, I ask her about her boyfriend, an English guy who she's been seeing since she met him on Tinder three years ago while "researching" dating apps.

"I'm seeing him after this trip," she swirls her wine. "We're going to Spain, then to Scotland."

"Do you ever get worried that it's mostly online? Like whenever you see each other, you're on vacation," I press. I think the relationship suits her for that reason, among others.

"I think one of us will end up moving in a couple years," she says. "I want him to move to the states."

Maybe that's true, Diana does have her younger sister to worry about. But I get the feeling she would move over here, too. I'm sure she's dying to use this piece to pitch a UK reality show once it airs. We finish off the bottle and go to bed early.

The following Monday, Jackie tells me what happened over the weekend. One of the sugar babies Diana cast got second thoughts after she'd already done the interview. Diana basically told her *it's a little late for that sweetie*, that we'd sue her if she tried to break her contract. Well, she called Diana's bluff and sent the contract to the reporter who immediately pulled the piece, vowing to never cover SeekingArrangement again. There goes another one. What is it with these sugar babies telling the truth? Don't they know that lying and faking it are essential sugar baby skills?

Chapter 46

Ten Years of SeekingArrangement

We're celebrating a decade of SeekingArrangement this year of our lord, 2016. The site was founded in 2006 by The CEO. He created the site because he had trouble with women growing up and thought, *what if they already knew how rich I am*? Insert SA, a site where a man's perceived success directly translates to hot women willing to date him, usually for a fee. But it's not prostitution, we swear!

We designed a three-tiered cake to celebrate this monumental decade of coercion and media coverage to be eaten at our holiday party at Top Golf. The cake gets wheeled out along with pretty girls toting strobe lights and letter signs that say R-E-F-L-E-X. The CEO goes in for his treasured speech moment. It's not a SeekingArrangement event without a toast from the man himself.

"I just want to thank all of you. Every year we have this Christmas party, and every year it gets bigger and bigger and bigger." He gestures with his hands. He's wearing his favorite beige sports coat and a skinny black scarf. "So here we are in our tenth year, thank you all. Without you, this would never happen. Thank you."

He keeps it short and sweet this time, and we clap and cheer because we know that's what he wants. Later I notice Zach, a sexy young man in a brown leather jacket, golfing in one of our bays. I've talked to him before at the office. I guess he's helping The CEO with some nutrition brand, but his only work experience is as a personal trainer. Jackie catches me checking him out.

"You know who that is, right?" she says, quietly so our coworkers can't hear.

"The CEO's pity hire of the moment?" I shrug.

"That's The CEO's sister's sugar baby." She smirks like someone who's got the hot gossip, which I guess she does.

It doesn't surprise me. The CEO always hires his sugar babies, and apparently now his sister's sugar babies, too. No wonder Zach is unskilled and yet somehow achieved a position of relative power. Classic sleeping with the boss's sister. How very on brand.

"Zach and Tara are living together in one of The CEO's units at Panorama Towers," Jackie says, raising her eyebrows.

Tara is The CEO's sugar baby, the one who was only nineteen at last year's holiday party. She's here somewhere.

"Are you serious?" I say, and double back to look at Zach again. "That's gross."

"It's the sugar baby trap house." She laughs, and so do I. She does have a few good zingers.

CHAPTER 47

THE FINAL STRAW

My sympathy is tested the following week when I have my annual review with Jackie. My trajectory is more media training for interviews, per my persistent requests. Then she tells me the financials and the math ain't mathing. I'm perplexed. I have not one but four jobs here with events, spokesperson, the *Let's Talk Sugar* website and my YouTube show, not to mention being called on for PR nonsense. I've increased my responsibilities and become the face of the brand, yet I'm making less in bonuses than last year and receiving the same petty cash raise. I try not to let my disappointment show. I spend the evening coming up with reasons for deserving more money, my presentation to Jackie, but she beats me to the punch.

[Dec 13, 2016, 9:16 AM]

Jackie: Hey let's go to lunch today. I've been thinking about your review and want to revisit some bonus and salary stuff. Let me know if you're free for lunch

Me: Okay thanks I appreciate it. That sounds good.

I see she's come to her senses, and she's already working on a breadstick when I arrive to meet her at Olive Garden. The waiter fills our glasses with Merlot, and Jackie breaks the news. First the good, which is that she wants to add another ten grand to my base. She also wants to give me "another ten grand on the top" for my bonus. I agree that's fair, but I was prepared to ask for less.

"Now the bad news," she says. "Diana is being let go. It's been a combination of things, but ultimately, she's just not the right fit," Jackie tells me, knowing it's not bad news for either of us.

"I see," I reply, trying not to give away my emotions. "That's interesting."

I'm not sure if I'm getting a raise to take on some of her responsibilities or just to keep me happy, and I don't care. The firing and the cash are long overdue. Without Diana obsessing over a reality show, we can reallocate resources. Maybe I can get some changes made to the website such as a process for removing bad actors. I chew on a breadstick and on my thoughts. Is Diana the lucky one? At least she's making it out alive.

PART FIVE
2017

Age: 25
Playlist: Hot Since 82, Tove Lo, Solardo
TV: *The Deuce, Big Little Lies, Queen of the South*
Favorite pastime: Partying, electronic dance music

CHAPTER 48

BROWN SUGAR AND DIAMOND KITTIES

There is a secret disparity on SA that we don't advertise but is well known in the community. Most sugar baby profiles are Black women. It's between forty and fifty percent. I'm not sure why this is the case, but I can surmise a few reasons. Statistically, women of color are vulnerable, less likely to have generational wealth. That makes them exactly the type of person who could truly benefit from a sugar daddy. Systemic problems make it more likely for them to turn to this lifestyle.

There's been a lot of issues on Seeking lately about what is and isn't considered racist. Is it racist to specify the ethnicities of women you're interested in? How about the ones you're not? How about "NO BLACK WOMEN PLEASE?" Is that racist and offensive? We are not qualified to be answering these questions, but we can throw a pop-up in Atlanta and hopefully win favor with a Black audience. It's a start, right?

"I'm actually glad the reporter isn't coming," Alexis smiles with her perfectly painted lipstick. "Less work for us!"

We're already at City Winery for our *Let's Talk Sugar* coaching event surrounded by sugar babies with their ears at the ready. With this news, we can be real with the girls, tell them to be careful because men on the site will lie to you to get in your pants, or defraud you and leave you broke and depressed.

"How can brown sugar babies stand out?" A thin woman with high cheek bones in a pink two-piece suit asks the question.

I let Alexis take this one. She's multiracial and has a way of putting these girls at ease. She's good at saying something soothing without saying much at all and certainly not revealing that racism and bigotry run rampant on SA and we have no way of stopping it. The sugar daddies are the ones paying, so they get to do pretty much whatever they want.

"Loving yourself is the most important thing you can do," she says. "Know what value you bring to the table. Maybe you're a great cook or a student with a fresh take on life. My advice would be the same for brown sugar babies as any others."

The following week, I click my loafers down the long hallway in the new office building. It used to be the location of the Nuclear Regulatory Commission, and we're left with strange residual safeguards that feel misplaced for a tech company. Narrow corridors flanked with private rooms, doors that automatically lock from the inside requiring key fobs to get out. Once when we didn't have key cards yet, I got locked in the auditorium. There in the dark under the fused bulbs and cathedral ceilings, I wondered why The CEO picked this place. Low price was obviously a factor, but I think he likes it. The secrets of SeekingArrangement need to be closely protected. I find Alexis behind her desk a few doors down from mine. Her eyes meet mine and they widen. She waves me in like she's fanning a flame on her shoulder.

"What happened?"

"Open your Slack," she says, shaking her head. "This is insane."

Our marketing chat is blowing up with news of a rumored sex cult out of Atlanta. Eight women were allegedly being held against their will in a mansion by a sugar daddy. Most of the women met him on (you guessed it) SeekingArrangement. Just when I thought I'd seen it all.

"I remember them."

I scan the story and recognize a particularly disturbing image. I recall an Instagram post Jackie sent me. The account posted a picture that went viral dubbing them the "Diamond Kitties." These eight girls are made up to look almost identical, all sitting at a dining room table wearing sunglasses, Birkin bags at the fore. Each has big fake boobs and similar hair. Two are twins. It appears to be a fake cult or something.

My skin crawls when I listen to a chilling 911 call from one of the women mentioning SeekingArrangement by name. Under the assumption of wealth and status SA touts, this guy was able to convince these women into being pimped, or sex trafficked to be more accurate. We find his account and peek at some of his thousands of messages to sugar babies. He was still recruiting just a couple days before his arrest. The reports against him are oddly specific, saying he wants to send sugar babies to another country for plastic surgery.

News about victims and their offenders meeting on SA is nothing new, but this one is a doozie. We take our lunches at our desks and quiet our socials, suspend all pitching. We may be numb to the horrors, but my heart still hurts for those girls.

That night, I'm restless, and I can't get the 911 call out of my head. I'm twenty-five now, and things are starting to look different. The older I get, the younger and younger these girls look. I used to put the onus on them to learn the evils of the world, the same way I did. Now I'm not so sure. For years, I've told myself I'm not responsible for what happens to people on SA. The site would be around with or without me, and I do the best I can to help the girls with *Let's Talk Sugar*. When you tell so many lies for long enough, it's hard to remember the truth.

CHAPTER 49

MEDIA TRAINING

We set up near the entrance of the massive auditorium. It's empty with dirty beige carpets and dark corners where bulbs need to be replaced. It feels haunted. The core PR staff is huddled around a small conference table, but not Jackie. She has more important things to deal with.

"Just remember, the reporter is never your friend. You are always on the record." Steve points at the air with his lanky finger, pacing in front of the rolling whiteboard.

This is Media Training 101. We're here to learn how to respond to the Diamond Kitties sex cult, and to the general tough questions. Journalists rarely go that deep, but if they do, we want to be ready. I've absorbed most of this in some of our other sessions, but I always want to hear Steve's wisdom. He's got to be eighty years old with decades of experience in a changing media landscape.

"Internal information needs to stay private," Steve says, knowing we've had issues with this in the past. "You have specific facts and figures, and you stick to only those. That's how you keep control of the narrative."

I chime in. "This reminds me of what you told us last time, something that stuck with me. We *should* be repeating the same things over and over to journalists. To us it will feel repetitive, but to the outside world it builds credibility."

The team nods and takes notes. *Say exactly what Brook says, check.* Both Jackie and The CEO see my potential; that's why I'm starting one-on-one training soon. I want to go into every interview and know that by the end of it, I can sway someone's opinion. I have faith in our PR team, but we're all inexperienced so mistakes are bound to happen.

Turnover at Reflex Media is sky high. New talent comes in with sexy salaries and brand-new MacBooks and quickly realize the toxicity. Many of them see this as a fertile ground for sowing the seeds of their own careers, since ascending the ranks here is easy. They don't need to have skills; they just need to be *there*. Stick it out longer than anyone else and they get *Senior* or *Manager* tacked onto their title with ten grand on the top. That is, if they don't quit or get fired first. The next phase of training is my favorite: interviews. As the most seasoned, I volunteer to go first. I sit under the hot lamp and smirk for the camera.

"What is SeekingArrangement?"

"Well first of all thank you so much for having me, and I'm so glad you asked," I say, looking him dead in the eye. "SeekingArrangement is a dating site just like any other, but our members are more open and honest about their expectations for a relationship."

I pretend every mock interview is real, and the camera adds to the illusion. It's all about word choice and inflection. *Open and honest* should stand out because that's what I want them to think I am. *Honest.* Next, I need to get the audience to like me. That's going to be hard, because I don't even like myself.

[Mar 24, 2017, 5:30 PM]

Jackie: We're going to come up with a 3 month one on one for you for rhetorical skills

Me: Cooooool love that

Jackie: Since you're our main spokesbabe

Me: Awesome ty

Jackie: I also am trying to wean The CEO off most interviews. So want to fully invest in you. How was it?

Me: Okay great. It was really good. I think we need The CEO there for help with some of the message about him.

CHAPTER 50

CUSTOMER SUPPORT

On one side, there's the sugar daddies. The wisdom of age and maybe some money gives them an advantage. On top of that, Seeking is tailored to give them the best experience possible and so continue to earn their $99 per month for a subscription. Better yet, anonymity is encouraged, so even if they do something deplorable, it's not necessarily associated with their identity.

On the other side are the sugar babies. Young and naive, varying from gullible to desperate. They usually have shame surrounding sex work and bury their bad experiences, like me. Some who do come forward to report incidents are turned away by law enforcement because they were soliciting or "asking for it" on a site like SeekingArrangement. Their only recourse is to report him directly on his profile.

I was under the impression we did something about it when we have evidence of repeat offenders; it's part of my whole PR spiel. Something like, "We do everything we can to protect our members. One member can report another for bad behavior, and bad actors get kicked off the site."

Imagine my surprise when I get an email from a sugar baby telling me to look into a sugar daddy profile saying he's assaulted multiple women he's met on the site and needs to be stopped. When I open his profile in admin, I'm shocked to see the counter at fifty-two next to his number of reports. *Fifty-two?*

Each one is worse than the last. Luring sugar babies with the promise of money, then drugging them in cheap hotel rooms or movie theaters. Harassing them endlessly to the point where some need to change their numbers. The acts he has been reported for get more and more brazen as I continue to scroll. *Why is this guy still on the site?* He must have slipped through the cracks.

I ask Jackie about it, and she says she doesn't know why he's still on the site, directing me to customer support. Usually, Seeking departments don't interact much, and everything is filtered through Jackie, but she's overworked and grants me more freedom internally to save herself time at this point.

She's been busy with the rebrand. SeekingArrangement is dropping "arrangement" altogether. We've already moved away from the word in our marketing and messaging, but this is official. The CEO bought the *Seeking.com* domain, new logos, and a new homepage. Recently, they also dropped the "expectations" section of the profile where sugar babies could list their price range using dollar signs, like on a Yelp page. Similar to a snake shedding its skin, we're always evolving at Seeking. A rebrand here, a change to our lingo there, shifting our public façade slightly into a more vanilla dating website over time. We have a member base of over ten million, and they know what's going on, or they'll learn quickly that the outward appearance is simply a front for an abysmal website that draws vulnerable women into sex work. So naturally, it's time for another rebrand.

The customer support office is behind a closed door, and they typically keep to themselves. Except for the manager, for most of them this is their first real job with healthcare and benefits. The pay is way more than they would make at any other customer support job. Last year, an older manager was hired to implement some processes. He's not in the office, so I ask one of the reps, an eighteen-year-old named Serena.

"Can you look up an account for me? He has fifty-two reports," I tell her, armed with the evidence on my laptop.

"What about him?"

"Why hasn't he been kicked off the site? Some of these are awful. He's drugging girls."

"Oh, we *used* to kick them off, but they would just make new profiles. Now they have to agree to the terms again. At least that way we can keep track when it's the same guy," she explains. "It saves time."

Unfortunately, it makes sense. Sugar daddies can easily make new accounts, so what's the point kicking them off? It's just an unpleasant user experience if the sugar daddy must make a new account, losing all his old messages and listing a new email address. Then he pesters customer support, making them less productive. They need to close these tickets; optimization is their goal. Why not save time *and* keep the sugar daddies happy? I mean they're the ones paying us.

"That's … interesting." I try to process. It doesn't behoove me to march up here and act like a bitch to these lower-level employees, but *it's fucked up.* "Does this happen a lot?"

"Oh yeah, some guys have hundreds," she says with a shrug.

Serena is just doing her job, and I'm just doing mine. So, we look at each other like two people just doing their jobs, bearing no burden of responsibility ourselves, and move on. It's moments like this when it's clear why Jackie doesn't often let the departments communicate.

CHAPTER 51

UNDERAGE DATING
AWARENESS WEEK

E arlier this year, an article about the pop-up I hosted in London came out. It featured photos of me on a private jet taken by an award-winning photographer. The article and the photos were arranged by *The Times of London* to accompany Lucy's story about me. I didn't love the story, but the pictures were fantastic and got a ton of likes on my Instagram.

The outlet covered our London *Sugar Baby Summit* back in May, publishing a lengthy story that details how underage girls can easily use the site by lying about their age. This is how all dating sites are. "Click here if you're over eighteen," no other safeguards in place. The article finds several accounts of underage sugar babies and tries to report them, but nothing happens. The journalist took the liberty of creating a fake sugar baby account using photos of her when she was fifteen. The profiles remain active, and Seeking allows it. It reads:

> "The next day with more pictures added to the profile, including two of her in a school uniform from when she was 15, our reporter found herself inundated with messages from men as old as 59. One user, who claimed to be a company director with a net worth of more than £1m and who thought she was 17, proposed to pay £150 for sexual services."

Bad for business? It's only bad if Seeking gets taken down or banned, which doesn't seem to be happening in any countries, despite repeated articles like this. Which makes it good for business. Men think they can easily find underage girls to pay for sex on Seeking, and they're right. More men than I ever realized prefer very young girls. Men like our fearless leader.

Interest in the dark side of sugar has skyrocketed following the articles. Since then, The CEO decided we needed to be more proactive in our attempt to deter the public from ousting us. His idea was to launch a somewhat ridiculous campaign. Introducing: "Underage Dating Awareness Week." Brilliant, right?

His childlike methodology reminds me of Trump. How could we be doing anything wrong when we have a whole campaign AGAINST underage dating? *See! Look over there!* The irony isn't lost on me. I can't begin to understand why calling attention to underage dating in this way would help our cause unless the recipient of the information is an absolute idiot. I can see the defense now, *"We would never allow underage sugar babies! See, we even created an AWARENESS WEEK! Not just a day, a whole week!"*

It's so fucking transparent it makes me sick. The ruse is another way to teach our members what is and what isn't allowed to be said on Seeking. In no way does that prevent them from doing the exact action we forbid on the platform; it just makes them smart enough to take those dalliances offline. It's not rocket science. Just make another email address, sign up for another account, and be careful not to get flagged for solicitation or being underage. *Wink wink, nudge nudge.* Carry on.

CHAPTER 52

DUBLIN

"They always want that new girl," I explain to a room full of Irish sugar babies. "They want that girl they can't get. That's why you shouldn't have sex on a first date."

The sugar babies eat it up, nodding and scribbling in their branded notebooks recycled from *Sugar Baby Summit*. The reporter isn't impressed. We're in a meeting room of a swanky hotel in Dublin fitted with crown molding and a tray of smoked salmon canapés. Rain bounces off the gray stone building. It hasn't stopped since we arrived in Ireland. Irish media is thirsty for content, and it has been relatively easy to score top tier placements here with our regular sugar baby coaching event pitch.

The interviewer is Vogue Williams, who I had never heard of until we arrived here. Apparently, she's a TV personality who's attempting hard-hitting questions for her new show. None of the sugar babies want to go on camera, but they're willing to speak to Vogue off-screen. One of them is only nineteen and concerned about losing her virginity to a man twice her age. I'm glad the cameras aren't rolling when she tells her story. When the crudités are lukewarm and the sugar babies have left, Vogue wants to have a chat with me alone.

"I don't really think it was an honest portrayal of what sugar dating actually is," she says.

She composes herself in a moment of pause that looks like she's stuck on freeze mode. When she looks up, I notice she's managed to make her eyes well with tears.

"I found myself getting really upset talking to one nineteen-year-old girl, and I feel upset now talking about it." Her voice cracks. "It's just so wrong."

I proceed into my best PR answer. SeekingArrangement is a choice, we do everything we can to keep members safe, etcetera. It's believable. But she's right. It's so wrong. Then again, I wouldn't be here if she wasn't willing to cover the website, popularizing and legitimizing the lifestyle by creating an entire episode of an "investigative" show centered around teenagers monetizing their sexuality on the internet. Who's more wrong? Me, who's trying to help them, or her, using their stories for her own gain?

The next day, Alexis and I pick up a copy of *The Irish Daily Star*, a local tabloid newspaper where there's a double page spread with our story. *"Life's so sweet when you date a sugar daddy,"* reads the headline with a full-page picture of me and a red-haired sugar baby holding a pink *Let's Talk Sugar* sign.

> "We are trying to give people the knowledge and skills, and the website tricks, to get the most traction and meet the most people possible," the article quotes me. "The site causes a lot of confusion, and we're here to diffuse that."

The TLDR: Seeking is a website where men can pay teenagers for sex with no legal ramifications and complete anonymity. I think we've made it clear, don't you?

[September 21, 2017, 5:47 PM]

To: press@seekingarrangement.com

Subject: SA Situation]

Hello my name is Khaliah. I hooked up with someone from SA about a year ago. It didn't end up going anywhere and he blocked my number. I ended up pregnant and had the child about 2 months ago but now I can't get in contact with the guy. I was wondering if SA could help me get in contact with the user please. I don't want to be a single mom.

CHAPTER 53

PARTY OF SEVEN

[Sep 27, 2017, 12:03 PM]

Me: Can you please task one of your girls to invite some girls The CEO thinks are hot from the waitlist? Or search through for the hot girls who bought tickets so we can introduce them to him

Alexis: Ok

Me: remember, anyone who looks under 18 and super skinny

Alexis: Ha I know

Me: I want to have a revolving door keeping him occupied

Alexis: Got it

[September 28, 1:10 AM]

The CEO: Are you and Alexis doing anything tomorrow? Can we meet for a late lunch or dinner?

7:38 AM

Me: Yes we can. Let me know if you want me to make a reservation.

"I wonder who's going to be at this dinner," I say to Alexis in our Uber heading to Philippe Chow, a restaurant The CEO chose. "Probably Tara or one of his other sugar babies."

We creep through traffic down the streets of Manhattan. I unbutton my pants to relieve my cramps. I'm so bloated, or maybe I caught a bug. The restaurant is unassuming from the outside, a punch of lemongrass and smoke hits me as we open the door.

"You're the first ones here," the hostess informs us. "Party of seven."

"*Seven?*" I spin toward Alexis. "Who the hell is going to be at this dinner?"

The CEO is so unpredictable. It might be a table of sugar babies, his lawyer-slash-best friend, the King of Morocco. We never know. Alexis and I are in town for another Seeking Party, this time at the ballroom at 230

Fifth Avenue. In walks The CEO with Tara and his two 80-something parents. *That's six …* I don't bother asking who the seventh is.

We are seated at a large table, Tara next to The CEO's mom, a woman with a thick scarf around her neck. I already know this is going to be the most awkward dinner of my life. That, and neither Alexis nor I are feeling very well after some questionable deviled eggs at lunch. But we couldn't say no to The CEO's invitation, and of course he wants to order the nine-course tasting menu.

To say the group has nothing to talk about is an understatement. I'm not sure The CEO's parents even speak English. Tara seems to be doting on the mother, making sure her tea stays filled. I do my best to make conversation, but it's too loud for them to hear, and The CEO is on his phone. I shovel soup dumplings into my mouth to avoid talking.

"Oh, Jessica's here," he says, getting up from his seat.

Tara shoots him a look, jaw dropped. I think we're all wondering the same thing. *Who's Jessica?* One of his business partners? Someone trying to con him? Usually, they're one in the same. Jessica is petite girl with blonde hair in a black faux fur shawl, probably twenty years old, and her face says it all. She was clearly not expecting to be having dinner with The CEO's parents, his PR managers, and his *other* girlfriend. I don't think he has the self-awareness to begin to understand that this is fucking weird. The CEO reminds me of an eight-year-old in a middle-aged man's body, and I think that's how he sees himself, too.

"Hi Jessica, nice to meet you!" I say, breaking ice since no one else is going to.

A baked Alaska flambés behind us as I force a sympathetic smile. She takes the empty seat next to The CEO. I eat another bite of Peking duck, chewing as slowly as I can.

Chapter 54

Seeking Mansion

"The CEO wants to be the next Hugh Hefner," Jackie says, showing off her new veneers. "He wants to buy a house and call it the *SA Mansion*."

I'm in her doorway eye level with her name plaque, the one she insisted on getting. *Vice President*. My laptop digs into my hip, and I feel a magnetism for anywhere but here. I resist the urge to avoid her, which I've gotten good at this year. I look back at Jackie whose index finger never seems to leave her computer's track pad.

"Excuse me? Please elaborate."

I take what Jackie says with a grain of salt as I take a seat across from her. She's been in a better mood lately, her divorce finalized. She has an older boyfriend of forty; she's thirty-two. Instead of using his name, she just calls him "the forty-year-old." I'm trying to be happy for her. She's come a long way from the Vanderpump Rules-obsessed PR manager I met in the dimly lit suite at the MGM four years ago, and not necessarily in a good way. Alexis told me that Jackie interfered with the results of our *Sugar Baby of the Year* calendar contest. A Black sugar baby won the votes, but Jackie assigned a different winner. A white one. I guess she didn't want a woman of color to be the winner three years in a row. Not what she wanted for the brand image, I guess.

"Sorry it's a mess," Jackie says, pushing her planner to the side to make a space for my computer.

"Don't be sorry, I know you're busy." I set it next to her venti tumbler. "Is the Hugh Hefner thing for another reality show?"

"Hopefully. Can you and Alexis go with him to house hunt?" she asks, gaze fixed on her laptop. The display is so small, I don't know why she never uses her monitor … or how she can focus with her screen so dirty.

One of The CEO's greatest aspirations is to be an executive producer on a reality show. A pipedream at this point. This concept is in line with his multiple girlfriends, plus Hefner passed away last week and perhaps he sees an in as a result. *The new Hef.*

"Sure, but it's a hard pass on the parties," I say and shake my head, my abdomen quivers. "Nothing with bedrooms, please and thank you."

I scan the Post-its on her whiteboard, some new workflow, and grab my computer. I can't be bothered to tell her how much I hate everything about this idea and this job in general, or risk her seeing it on my face.

"I know, it's crazy. Just go with it," she says as I find the exit to flee. "I feel like you're going to write a book about this one day," she lets out a breathy laugh.

"Maybe," I say, trailing off down the hall.

[Oct 12, 2017, 12:53 PM]

Jackie: (Screen shot of a text message with The CEO)

> ***The CEO***: *I already got it. Just not available until jan 1st. The day I broke up with Tara is the day the seller said yes to my offer. New beginning*
>
> ***Jackie***: *Congrats?*
>
> ***The CEO***: *Yes happened yesterday. It's officially over. Too much drama in my life.*
>
> ***Jackie***: *Good, I'm glad.*

Jackie: So you know I don't just make things up. Hopefully it sticks this time

Me: Gasp!

CHAPTER 55

#MeToo

Twitter is in a frenzy with *#MeToo*. The CEO wants to make a statement but luckily, we talk him down. What would Seeking have to contribute to a conversation about sexual harassment when the website directly causes the mistreatment of women? It's best if we stay out of it.

Reading the tweets with a lump in my throat, I feel a sense of familiarity I can't place. It's visceral, watching the masses band together trying to make change happen with their voices. I'm reminded of the stories from sugar babies over the years, the ones about abuse and victimization. Are we on the wrong side of history? We tout the site as a grand equalizer for women, shrinking the wealth inequality gap when rich men give poor girls money, the Disney version of events.

The victims know Seeking is full of predators, having experienced it firsthand. Because it's sex work, sugar babies are often dismissed and stripped of their right to rectify their situations. It might be too late for legal ramifications, but it's not too late to use their combined voices. The culture of shame and secrecy keeps victims silent … but what if they weren't? What if the victims came forward in a viral moment like *#MeToo*? Internally, we have no idea about the rate of victimization through Seeking. Everyday? Every hour? Every *minute*?

Individually, they're just deleted comments, unanswered emails, and sad whispers with a subpoena sprinkled in now and again. But data doesn't lie. Cultivation of voices is the only way the picture can come into focus, a data point that can't be deleted from a server. Together, the victims could knock this house of cards down in one breath.

PART SIX
2018

Age: 26
Playlist: Bicep, Four Tet, Gorgon City
TV: *Shameless, 90 Day Fiancé, Riverdale*
Favorite pastime: Traveling, disassociating, drugs

CHAPTER 56

MOVING ON UP

The CEO's office is nothing special – bare white walls, corner window, and sort of L-shaped – with only the visitor chairs visible through the glass door. It's like you can see who's in the principal's office, but not the principal himself. He's out of sight at his desk, and I never know if he's inside unless I knock and wait for an answer.

Jackie put in her resignation last month. Something about launching her own firm. To break the news, she took her favorite managers, me included, out to a nice dinner at Joe's Stone Crab. Before resigning, she fired Peg. Then the CTO quit. Something about a Bitcoin wallet fortune. And the kicker: Jackie and the CTO had been carrying on an affair for months, negotiating large bonuses before their departures. *He* was the mysterious "forty-year-old" she had been talking about.

The CEO's desk is strewn with stacks of papers and files, printouts, magazines, and books. He calls me in for a one-on-one meeting, so I'm sitting in the hot seat behind the glass door that feels like a microscope slide.

"As you know, there's been a restructuring. Managers will now report to me, and we will all have a meeting every Wednesday at five thirty," he says, promptly distracted.

I hear the buzz on his desk, freezing my energy and strategic responses until he's finished the text. That's how we act around The CEO, suspended in time until we can be of service. His phone keyboard clicks are on, so I can hear every letter of his response. He sets down the phone, and the titanium frame clinks onto the white desk.

"I also want to ask you about PR. Why do you think the quality has gone down?" he asks, furrowing his signature oily brow and tilting his head. "We used to get CNN and talk shows, where are those?"

He's right, but it has nothing to do with the PR staff. The sugar stories are tired from being rinsed and repeated. Media interest has dried up, or they're holding out for our *Sugar Baby Summit* event in New York this April.

"That's a good question," I reply, trying to channel Jackie, remembering the ways she taught me to sway The CEO in my favor.

"Do you think you could lead the PR team?" he asks, a question I didn't expect. "And Alexis could lead the content team?" *Wait, what?* The CEO wants to switch us out as though we're interchangeable.

"I think I could lead both teams," I say with a note of ambivalence. I don't want to be stuck back in PR. It's vapid and would make my success too measurable.

"Okay," he replies, and I know I've said the wrong thing. "Well thank you."

"No problem!" I take my cue and get up to leave. He wanted me to love his idea, but I've never been one to give in to his antics.

"By the way, I'm having some of the managers over to my house on Saturday. I want you to come," he says.

I take in a deep breath and nearly run down the stairs. The CEO sucks up the oxygen in every room, and as soon as I leave, I can breathe. This is the second time he's invited me to his new place on a weekend. I made up an excuse last time, but I think I need to go this time if I want to keep favor with him. I'll go if Alexis goes. Misery loves company.

CHAPTER 57

THE SEX WORKER

Valerie lives at Veer Towers, a high-rise nestled between Aria and Crystals on the Las Vegas Strip. Her floor to ceiling windows overlook the roundabout and water feature near the valet. The place belongs to a client of one of Valerie's friends. She and the friend are both sex workers.

Valerie recently moved from Seattle and was introduced to me one night while I was out partying, which I've been doing more of these days. It's a nice escape from the darkness of my job. When I learned Valerie is a sex worker, I knew we'd be fast friends. She invited me over, so here I am in her living room admiring her plants and craft supplies. I circle around a silver stripper pole to seat myself on her impressive green velvet couch.

"You don't have a TV?" I imagine it might be a part of her new age Seattle persona.

"I just watch shows on my laptop," she says, adjusting each breast in her crop top, studying her reflection in her full-length mirror. "I think it looks better without one, like for in-calls," she looks back at me, maybe searching for my approval.

We're about the same age, but she seems young. She likes to play Animal Crossing on her Nintendo DS and dreams of a *Pretty Woman* plotline for her life. I'm a bit more jaded at this point in my pursuit of a tolerable patron, but Valerie does have a few things figured out. She used Backpage for years, but decided to stop when she was finding enough clients through Twitter and word of mouth.

"I don't want to become reliant on Backpage because it could get shut down. I'm having a photoshoot soon. I need more content," she says, scrolling through her own Instagram pictures, zooming on one with two fingers.

Clearly, we follow the same news. Her stage name is Charlie, her dominant alter ego. Charlie spends all day texting with lonely men and setting up pricey meetings. Once a month she goes to the Moonlite Bunny Ranch brothel to work legally.

"They make you stay for a week at a time," Valerie explains of the ranch. "They treat the girls like shit, and the owner beats some of them." She shakes her head and her red hair falls from behind her ear, a bob that frames her round face.

"Do you know this girl?" I ask, pulling up a blog post from the Bunny Ranch's website.

Recently *Vice* quoted this post as a counter to my interview in a story about *Let's Talk Sugar*. It's been causing a moment within the online sugar baby community. It reads:

> Online platforms such as Seeking Arrangement, which host millions of eager sugar babies and sugar daddies/mommies, are simply pimping schemes that admit no responsibility for their users' safety. The legal distinctions that separate sugar babies and illegal prostitutes are flimsy, and sugar websites get away with offering what they do by promoting the fantasy that sugaring is so entirely different from prostitution when it is exactly that – prostitution. The distinct problem with sugar websites – when things go awry – is that they overtly promote a farce and take no responsibility, consequently rendering all parties involved infinitely vulnerable.

"I've never seen her," Valerie says, skimming the article on my phone. "I've done stories before too," she says. "I did a Reddit AMA that sort of went viral," she shrugs, glancing up to check my reaction.

"Would you ever do press for Seeking? Like as a legal sex worker?" I ask. "I'm looking for experts for a conference I'll be hosting this April, in New York."

"I'd love to! I've never been to New York." Her eyes light up like a slot machine.

I'll need to clear it with Alexis, but she would be the perfect addition to my roster of speakers for *Sugar Baby Summit*. Having a sex worker explain the difference between sugaring and sex work is the ideal way to double down on this narrative. It's brazen. The CEO will love it.

"So Seeking is basically like the girlfriend experience?" she asks, referring to a style of escorting where the sex worker is more doting and acts like she truly likes the man, usually for overnight visits.

"Pretty much," I reply. I don't mention that phrase – along with other sex worker lingo – is banned from the Seeking website. She just needs a little coaching.

CHAPTER 58

BRITISH DOCUMENTARY

I peer down from Aqua Shard – a restaurant atop the tallest building in London – to the tube station below. The train lines look like glowing veins traveling to an alien hub. It's the perfect place to host a roomful of would-be sugar babies. A sweet Russian hostess in all black leads us to our private dining room.

"You're here for SeekingArrangement?" she asks me. She must be a sugar baby.

"Yes, we're here for a *Let's Talk Sugar* event," I begin, wondering how she figured it out. "Are you on the website?"

"Yes." She flashes a shy smile and with a long sweep of her sculpted arm beckons us toward our suite.

Alexis and I are here to shoot for a British documentary. As per usual, I'm all about optics and aerial views for my events. I'm literally and metaphorically looking down on the world. Looking down my nose on society for being judgmental, looking down on traditional sex workers who give sugaring a bad rep, and looking down from a modern dining experience on townies below.

"You've really outdone yourself this time," Alexis says, marveling at the breathtaking setup.

It's a fishbowl with glass walls and three round tables. The room feels like a viewing chamber, perfect for observing animals in their natural habitat. Sugar babies at a luxury establishment with glasses of bubbly certainly fit the bill. The girls trickle in, all of whom are paid and willing to appear on camera. Most of them are only willing to be extras, with a select few giving interviews for an additional fee. The girls we cast seem younger and younger to me these days, and in the UK, they *are* younger since the legal drinking age is only eighteen.

"We're expecting fourteen," Alexis says, checking each one off on her Notes app as they arrive.

"We'll be lucky if ten show up," I reply.

When most of the sugar babies are seated, Alexis leans over their shoulders to quietly remind them of the rules: No talking unless you're called on, no saying you've been paid for sex, and deny being paid to be here. All questions will be submitted on a piece of paper then answered aloud. The film crew sets up a huge camera and lights in the corner pointed at the round sugar baby tables dotted with lychee martinis and pretzel bread.

"We're going to get started in a minute." I call to the girls like a school-teacher getting students to settle down.

"Can I have another lychee martini?" a tanned sugar baby with over-stuffed lips and stringy blonde extensions asks. Hot pink lipstick coats the rim of her glass that's been emptied after a few gulps. She shoots me an entitled glare like she knows my secret and has me wrapped around her finger.

"I'll have one too!" Another sugar baby says, and like popcorn they all want another lychee martini at £24 each.

"Take your time with the martinis," I whisper to the waiter, and then turn to the group for my on-camera intro. "Thanks everyone for coming," I say. "I know you have a lot of questions about the sugar world, and I'm here to answer them."

Having me speak is only a formality. The sugar babies can barely hear me anyway, and the producers mostly want to interview them. We shuffle the production team out the door once they've gotten what they need so we can settle with the sugar babies privately. They're paid on the spot with envelopes of cash. Half now, half when the piece comes out. The bill comes to me, and it's over £4,000, £800 in fucking lychee martinis. The sugar babies are wasted. One can barely walk with legs like a baby deer. She tells me she's only nineteen and that she's sorry.

"Can we get one more lychee martini?" the inflated-lip sugar baby slurs as I close out the check.

"No," I peer at her over my glasses. "No more lychee martinis," I say, staring her straight in the eye. Her false eyelash is hanging on by a thread, and so is my patience. *Production is gone, bitch. You're cut off.*

CHAPTER 59

THE VEGAS PARTY

When people find out Seeking is based in Las Vegas, they say, *that makes sense.* There's a common misconception that sex work is legal in Vegas, encouraging lonely men at the Flamingo to call GIRLS DIRECT TO YOU off the side of that red mobile billboard, the same one I've seen since I was a kid. Most people who grew up here want to get out and away from the infectious gluttony it breeds. Am I a product of my environment?

Internally, we've considered a party in Vegas, but it never made sense with our media agenda since there aren't any national outlets here for coverage. The CEO floated the idea to me last year as being in line with his new goal to be "the next Hugh Hefner." We don't allow cameras or the press at our parties anymore. It's too risky. Both for the members, and for us. No one wants the evidence recorded.

Sixty floors above The Strip, I take the last few moments to myself before the charade begins. I get a text from The CEO and my blood boils. I used to get a sinking feeling when I saw his name in my notifications, now it feels more like rage. I grip my phone and grit my teeth. A few staff bustle around, scanning the bar and photobooth for last looks. Thankfully I'm not on my own anymore; I found a new event coordinator after the first one I hired had a mental breakdown within three weeks. I had to let her go.

"Is this the SA party?"

I hear a voice call from behind me, and I shudder. It belongs to a lone sugar daddy, waiting by the elevator holding five small Cartier gift bags. He's standing next to a six-foot-tall retractable banner that suggests this is the masquerade he seeks.

"Indeed. Are you at one of our VIP tables?" I ask. If he doesn't have one, he'll feel like maybe he should buy one, and if he does, I can tell him to have a seat. He's early.

"Yes, I'm Steve, I bought one last night. I just happened to be in town."

I'm *sure* he did. Lots of men came to Las Vegas specifically for this event. It's essentially a legal sex party above a casino, ideal for married daddies. They can say they're in town for a conference. It's their *Eyes Wide Shut* fantasy come to life. Steve isn't wearing a mask, which means he's rich enough not to care who sees him.

"You're the first one here," I say, kind of hoping he gives me one of the bags. "Let me show you to the tables, and you can pick yours."

Ping … the elevator doors open and out steps a couple. One of them says something in a Midwest accent. They gawk at the provocative signage and the man with five tiny gift bags.

"We're closed for a private event." I say and shoo them back into the elevator. "Sorry, our security detail isn't installed yet," I say to Steve while leading him to the mezzanine.

I drop him off in the VIP and wave down the cocktail waitress. "There's a very rich man in the VIP for you," I tell her with a wink.

The party fills up with the regular variety of masked patrons, eyes darting, drinks empty, looking for whoever they might find. It's the typical crowd – mostly young women and men over forty – with a little less clothing and a little more gusto. At one point, a sugar baby is straddling a man in the corner for a full on make out session. Then I realize … she's an employee. One of The CEO's random hires, I think she's a lawyer.

I wait for a particularly long time for one of the single bathrooms and knock on the door to emphasize my point. Maybe someone accidentally locked it from the inside. A minute later a scantily clad sugar baby with red lipstick smeared around her chin and tousled hair emerges and scurries past. I pause before pushing the door open. A bald man in a Zorro mask wearing a shit-eating grin pops out. I gasp, take a step back. My chest tenses. Inside the bathroom, I find a face print smudged on the window, same red lipstick. It feels like the scene of a crime. I take a long drag from my vape and wait for it to dissipate, staring down at the neon signs below. I wipe away the evidence with a damp paper towel, squeezing it in my fist to stop myself from punching the glass. *This is too much.* I make my rounds, heading up to check on Steve and the VIP daddies. Alexis is at the base of the stairs typing on her phone.

"How's it going over here?" I ask.

"It's good. The guy with the Cartier bags is enjoying himself," she says, glancing around the room. "I'm looking for short Latina girls for one of the other daddies."

I pop up the stairs and notice one of the sugar babies is bent over the booth donning only a G-string, showing off her butt. She looks very intoxicated. Alexis swoops in, b-lining for G-string girl.

WINK, WINK, NUDGE, NUDGE

"Put your damn clothes on," she says. "Girl, get your shorts." She gently grabs the girl's arm to make it clear she means *now*.

The sugar baby looks around without making eye contact. "Oh sorry, Steve gave it to me." She laughs and snaps the red thong against her hip. I guess that's what was in the bags.

"You need to keep your clothes on," Alexis reiterates calmly. She's familiar with the audacity of these sugar babies after years of handling them. She takes a deep breath and watches to make sure G-string girl finds her pants. "Can you help me find petite Latinas?" she asks. "My feet are killing me."

"Of course," I tell her, and head off on my side mission.

When the clock mercifully strikes 2:00AM in thirty minutes, the guests will become the resort's problem. I need to sneak out before leftover sugar babies migrate to the casino floor like a mob of hungry wolves. There are never enough sugar daddies to go around.

CHAPTER 60

THE SPEAKER RETREAT

After each *Sugar Baby Summit*, we evolve. Filling in the cracks where the truth shines through has been a trial-and-error process. Between wrangling journalists, coercing sugar babies, and hosting what is calculated to give the impression of a professional event, things tend to go awry. But not this time. We're covering all our bases by throwing money at it with a huge conference space on Columbus Circle and prior in-person coaching for each speaker. Our experts are successful sugar babies, a couple daddies, influencers, and therapists. I wanted to get a celebrity like a Real Housewife, but nothing has panned out. I'm flying them out for a "speaker retreat" where we'll size them up and teach them how to lie to media. Who poses the biggest risks? What will they say when the questions get tough?

"I just want to thank everyone for taking time out of their busy lives to be here today," I say, standing at the head of the boardroom table.

The speaker's heads all turn to me in unison, but I look past them out a window at the far side of the room overlooking steam funnels and a mob of honking cars. It's a rented meeting space for our program in the same swanky hotel we're all staying at, off Lexington Avenue. I just want to get back to my room; I'm watching *Stranger Things* on Netflix.

"*Sugar Baby Summit* is about empowering sugar babies to own their relationships and be proud of sugaring." I advance my slide. "Part of why you're here now is to help you be absolutely prepared, to bolster your own credibility."

After the roster introduces themselves, we take headshots and videos for social media. Then each speaker receives a thirty-minute, one-on-one media coaching session to go over appropriate answers as defined in their contract. We're very careful to protect ourselves with legal threats, but hardly consider protections for our members.

The speakers keep asking about The CEO, and for dinner they get to meet him. He finds the group in a private dining room along the Hudson, three sugar babies trailing behind him. Tara isn't one of them. There's Jessica from the dinner with his parents; Zoe, his live-in Las Vegas girlfriend;

and one I have not yet met, with mousey brown hair and big gasses. It's hard to keep up.

The next morning, I meet Alexis in the hotel lounge for a coffee before we Uber to the airport. We're sitting at a highboy table with a view of the street below, bumper to bumper traffic and sirens wailing in the distance.

"Aren't you heading straight to South by Southwest?" Alexis asks. She knows I'm going to the tech conference in Austin, Texas. I nod. "The CEO told me he didn't think I should go." She shrugs and swirls her coffee. "I'd rather spend the week away from him anyway."

"Yeah, he told me the same thing. But I've wanted to go for years, so screw him," I say between bites of a chocolate croissant. "I'm excited." I notice a faint noise – someone yelling on the street beneath us – through the single pane windows. "Is that a fight?"

I watch an emotional blonde-haired girl who is crying, struggling, and shouting at a man inches from her face. He grabs her forearm. She squirms, manages to break free, then runs across the street into oncoming traffic. The man takes off after her, horns blaring.

"That's Zoe!" Alexis says.

Our jaws drop and I nearly spit out my coffee while my eyes track the spectacle down the opposite sidewalk past yellow cabs and fire escapes. It's like a scene from a schoolyard where a young boy and girl are playing chase, only darker. My chest pinches when I realize we know them. Not only that, but the man who was trying to restrain her is The CEO. *My boss.*

"No *way!*" I squint. "Fuck. It's definitely them."

The CEO catches up to her and grabs her shoulders. His lips are moving, and I imagine him trying to console her, maybe. I wonder what she's so upset about. She was probably gaslit, lied to, and made to feel like she was crazy by a man nearly thirty years older. I wish I could shake her out of it. Tell her what I wish I'd known when I was twenty years old. These men are manipulating us, I'd say. Would she listen? Would I have listened? I cram the remainder of my pastry into my mouth and try not to wonder.

CHAPTER 61

SXSW

The streets are blocked for the festival, so I'm dropped off around the corner from Russian House, the restaurant The CEO chose for tonight. His ex-wife is Ukrainian, so I guess he has a taste for Eastern European cuisine. As per usual, I'm not sure who's coming, I'm not even sure who else is in town. We're in Austin for South by Southwest, the annual conference and festival for techies and musicians.

A 9:00PM reservation is late for me, but I've never had Russian food, so it will be a memorable meal if nothing else. There are costumes in the entryway of the restaurant, a thick fur coat, a military hat with an iron cross. I suppose this is for patrons to get in character. This place is straight out of the Soviet Union. In walks The CEO with Zoe. They are in matching brown jackets. She's petite with a physique typical of his tastes. I offer her a hug, and she accepts. I always make nice with The CEO's sugar babies since they may eventually do press for me.

"You look so cute!" I say, and she does, flare pants and a sort of hippie aesthetic.

The pair are followed by Wayne, the lawyer, and his wife, whose name I immediately forget. Wayne is handsome, tall with salt and pepper hair, and a confident air; his wife is a conventionally beautiful woman in her late twenties. They met on *WhatsYourPrice*, sister website of Seeking. From what I understand, Wayne is an investor in Seeking, our legal counsel, and The CEO's BFF.

"We're having a problem with Sharon," The CEO says across the table, looking at a Slack message on his phone. "She's a no-call no-show today."

Sharon is a young attorney The CEO hired, the one who made out with a sugar daddy at the party, extra sloppy. I don't know much about her, other than she's staying in the unit formerly known as the sugar baby trap house since Tara and Zach moved out.

"Should I have the building staff check on her?" he asks, looking at me.

"I would. This sounds like grounds for termination."

I dollop sour cream into my borscht. The food is delicious. Pelmeni dumplings, beef stroganoff. While I stir my soup, I stir the pot, keeping the attention off myself. People at the office already don't like Sharon, but I'm curious what Wayne thinks of her, him being the actual legal counsel.

"I would agree, but either way you should have someone check on her. We don't want to make any assumptions," Wayne says, and I'm almost certain he hates her.

After a few rounds of vodka shots, The CEO mentions that Zoe got mad at him for something earlier in the day, an aside to another story about his dissatisfaction with the conference sessions. He was late to a keynote and wasn't let in since there weren't any more seats. This has infuriated him.

"We bought the VIP tickets, so we should get VIP access," he whines.

I'm stuck on the Zoe issue. She's been quiet, hunched over on her phone all night. She usually doesn't say much, but she's been despondent for over an hour.

"So why did you get mad at him?" I ask softly.

She glances up and wrinkles her chin. "I searched for my name in his text messages, and he was talking about me," she says, shooting him the side eye.

"Oh wow, I've never thought to do that. I guess you went looking and you found something," I say, knowing she likely went snooping without permission.

"I guess," she sighs, and continues scrolling on Instagram.

The following night, The CEO wants to meet at a rustic Western restaurant boasting a wood-fire oven. The air inside smells smoky and sweet with hints of whiskey. I order a chardonnay and wait for the guest of honor to arrive, parking myself near the natural stone fireplace beneath antler chandeliers. I'm surprised when The CEO shows up without Zoe. Instead, he's with the other sugar baby from the speaker retreat, the mousey girl of maybe twenty-two. A while back he told me he wants to have blonde *and* brunette girlfriends. They are both still wearing their SXSW badges. Hmm … I wonder what happened to Zoe, and if that's her badge around the other girl's neck. I choose not to ask.

The next day I'm in the Austin airport waiting for my flight back home, and I get a call from Valerie. "I quit the Bunny Ranch," she says. "The owner is such a prick, even after all I've done for them."

"So how are you going to work?" I ask. That was the angle for *Sugar Baby Summit*: a *legal* sex worker. Does this still fit my narrative?

"I'm doing in-calls," she says, the term for hosting men at her place. It's not exactly legal or safe, but that's her choice.

"Okay, well you know the reason we wanted to have you was because you were working at The Ranch. Without that, you're in a compromising position putting your name in the press."

"I can use another name," she offers.

"I don't think that matters, you could still get in trouble. I think we'll have to pull you." I'm almost relieved. Maybe it was arrogant of me to put her on anyway. Everything happens for a reason.

"Okay I get it," she says, obviously disappointed. "I still want to go … as a sugar baby."

"We'd love to have you," I say, and it's true. "I'll send you a ticket."

"Okay. Thank you," she says, and the energy between us shifts.

At the end of the day, Valerie is a sugar baby, just as unreliable and chaotic as the rest. I need to keep these girls at a distance in case any shit hits the fan.

CHAPTER 62

FOSTA

I pull into the parking lot around 9:00AM and swerve my car beneath a row of palm trees long overdue for a trim. A few wily cacti beneath the windows catch my eye. I glance at the Reflex Media logo across the top of the building. The CEO was proud of the signage once it was installed. He loves little symbols of prestige. His white Mercedes coupe is parked in his unofficial spot, front and center to the walkway. He's here early.

Walking toward my reflection in the glass, I hear the click of my loafers. They're part of my new look. Dressing more professionally helps me believe my own lies and forget that I'm rotting inside. I boop my key fob on the receiver and pull open the door. Wayne is in the foyer, idle on the linoleum, a stack of files in hand.

"Oh good, you're here. Do you have time to talk?" he asks.

This is the first time he's asked to meet with me privately, and I know why. The FOSTA-SESTA bill reached the Senate and passed, ending Backpage, an online marketplace for sex workers and a known hub for traffickers. We've been expecting this ruling, and the anxiety has led to mania internally over rushed changes to Seeking's interface.

FOSTA-SESTA is now an amendment to Section 230, a correction of sorts to an outdated provision. Section 230 is a protection policy for websites, created in 1996 before Congress fully understood the internet and what it would become. At the time it was enacted, AOL had only been around a few years. In 1996, there were twenty-six words added to our laws:

> No provider or user of an interactive computer service shall be treated as the publisher or speaker of any information provided by another information content provider.

Seemingly innocuous, right? This phrase basically means that websites are not legally responsible for the content their users post, but also ends up absolving dating website operators of legal liability for crimes between their members. I mean, it's not the website's fault … right? Backpage and

Seeking supposedly function in a legal "gray area" where there is lots of money to be made. FOSTA-SESTA changes that caveat, in effect shutting down Backpage and codifying their culpability in sex work and sex trafficking despite Section 230's protections. If applied to Seeking, the policy would shut us down too.

This is why we're always altering something – a rebrand, a new domain, new terms, removed dollar signs, and on and on – day after day. The changes are small enough to not deter our core member base, while subtle enough to code as more of a typical dating site over time. With the passage of this new law, the obfuscation must reach new heights.

I find Wayne in a small, windowless meeting room with sterile white paint, a white table, and a whiteboard across one side. I take a seat and open my laptop, open my spokesperson notes. Canned answers, phrasing, pivots. I keep a sort of FAQ for the PR staff so we can coordinate messaging and articulate half-truths.

"I know you've already been briefed on this, but I want to talk through a couple scenarios and get your take," he says, hands folded across his belly.

Within the walls of Seeking, the Backpage fiasco has been a blueprint for what we want to avoid. Backpage was accused of "coaching" users on how to avoid behavior associated with sex trafficking of minors, among other nefarious nudges. In some ways, Seeking does the same thing, holding seminars and making users agree to "Terms of Use." Seeking issues a slap on the wrist when rules are broken, molding member behavior online, but certainly not offline.

"I have no doubt you're prepared for questions. Your interviews are great. I'm more interested in your philosophy," he says.

Wayne doesn't understand sugaring the way I do, the member's motives and beliefs. It's a bit of a puzzle, the sugar world. A man who's willing to pay for sex, but doesn't see it as prostitution, meets a young lady who simply wants to be "spoiled." Where's the crime?

"Now *that* is interesting." Wayne leans back in his chair and looks up at the ceiling tiles, a few bearing brown liquid stains from leaks after a heavy rain. "If neither the sugar baby nor the sugar daddy thinks they're participating in sex work, then technically they aren't."

While we might be able to defend ourselves against the burning questions, that's not the glaring problem I see with Seeking. The issues with the website are degenerate enabling acts that are indefensible. People want the same answers to the same curiosities. Is it? Or isn't it? Are they, or are they not? If you ask me, those are the wrong questions. The layer of bullshit surrounding this company is so foul I can smell it, or maybe someone left old food in the fridge. I'm glad to see this legislation. There are reasons why it's flawed as laws usually are, sometimes hurting the ones they claim to help protect. Still, it's a step in the right direction. I'll watch the empire burn from the inside. The stratagem can't last much longer.

I want to leave, believe me. My frustration keeps me up at night; it's making my hair fall out. But I've stupidly set myself up with an expensive life and I can't afford to switch jobs and take a huge pay cut. For now, I need to stack my shiny pennies and prepare my exit plan while seething and biting my tongue in the office. *Sugar Baby Summit* is next week, the result of over a year of planning and persuasion. After that, I'm taking time off to clear my head. Croatia, then Spain with a group of partiers and a vile of acid. The trip is paid for partially by Yousef, who still buys me things here and there. It's the least he can do.

Chapter 63

Sugar Baby Summit 2018

My Louboutins clack against the pavement and a brisk wind cuts up my dress, nearly knocking me and my *Let's Talk Sugar* cutout to the ground. I use the cutout as a sail and recalibrate my balance. I cannot fuck up these expensive shoes. It's a brisk April morning on Columbus Circle. The team pulls up behind me following my near miss, my blunder with mother nature.

"Are you ready to get this over with?" I say to Alexis while we remove our coats and send them through the x-ray machine.

She laughs and continues typing an email on her phone, presumably wrapping up a loose end. "More than you will ever know," she smiles. "There is so much press, Brook, I'm having to turn people away."

"Consider this the most exclusive event in town."

I remind her of our latest tactic: tell them they can't have the story, and they'll want it even more. Gatekeeping turns the press into sugar fiends. In a luxury conference space on the tenth floor, our merry band of PR misfits funnel in beneath thirty-foot ceilings past abstract sculpture art. We're finally in a space that makes sense for *Sugar Baby Summit*. Five separate rooms in which to cordon our various esteemed guests, essential for the logistics of our media manipulation. Keep everyone separate.

With radios in their ears like the fucking secret service, the PR team orchestrates a grand dance around journalists and producers. The outlets get to interview only the ones who PR staff permit. Controlled, contrived, and covert. Everything is down to the letter, so the resulting news pieces will reflect sugaring in the image we provide. Deception built on lies compounded over the years has formed a permanent knot in my gut. I keep reminding myself, two more weeks and I'll be on a plane to Europe.

I put an earpiece in, listen to the chatter, then ditch the walkie in our staff hideaway room. I have a pounding headache, and my feet are already sore. I pop a couple Advil and take a long drag of my vape pen in a secluded corner near the kitchen. I hear the distant rumblings of sugar baby attendees down the expansive halls. I need to be ON for the next five hours.

"We have a situation," Alexis whispers in my ear. "There's a student journalist trying to sneak in. He's been talking shit on Twitter, so I told him he had to leave."

"Not him again." I know exactly who she's referring to, a scrawny character who's been tweeting about how he's going to expose us. Not very sly.

"I'm going to give security and staff his description so we can kick him out if he tries to come back," she says, holding down the button on the receiver like an army general going to war.

Between vape hits and coffee breaks, I'm a shell of a person all day. On autopilot, dragging around a human meat suit. I've become so good at dissociating from this job, it's my default now. I strike a pose for the cameras, smile for the sugar babies, and hide from anyone who wants to have an honest conversation. There in the back hallway, eyes closed, sensibilities exhausted, I pray for my head to stop throbbing. I've got to get away from this job. The longer I'm entrenched in these monstrous acts, the more of a monster I become.

Chapter 64

Virginity For Sale

Fractures in Seeking's story, our story, pop up every day. A shocking article here, a seedy exposé there. It's like that kid's game, *Don't Spill the Beans*. Bean after bean, lie after lie, we pile them one on top of the other until … BOOM! The pile comes crashing down. The dam of secrets can't possibly hold forever. The morning after *Sugar Baby Summit*, Alexis pings me a news story out of Atlanta. The title reads: *"Businessman accused of raping teen he met on sugar daddy website."* Fucking fantastic.

> A Memphis businessman is accused of raping a 17-year-old he met on a dating website that describes itself as the "leading Sugar Daddy dating site." The teenager told investigators she met Wayne Giannini on the dating website "Seeking Arrangement," and that they were involved in a "consensual sexual relationship" for several months, but eventually she said she felt threatened. The 52-year-old is also charged in two additional pending rape cases.

Only two pending rape cases? A guy like that has likely been on Seeking for years, mistreating dozens, or even hundreds, of victims. Stories like this break all the time, and we rarely make public comment. What is there to say, other than *whoopsies, our cracks are showing?* She pings me again a few hours later with another story. This one is worse than the last: *"Virginity for sale: How 'sugar babies' site that claims it just offers 'honest' dating is revealed as an auction for women's innocence."*

Yikes. Alexis briefed me on the topic, but luckily I didn't get any questions from the journalists at the summit. She let The CEO handle those interviews, protecting me and our coaching event endeavors. There have been plenty of underage sugar baby stories, but auctioning virginity is a new low. Just like Backpage, we have some phrases that are not allowed in profiles. This will likely result in a new flagged phrase: *virgin*. This is the worst story I've seen in a long time. The more depraved the story, the more likely it is that demented fake sugar daddies join the site. I wish the media would understand that. I'm just glad the *Daily Mail* didn't use any photos of me or mention my name. Even so, I know I'm on thin ice. And it's cracking.

CHAPTER 65

THE DOCTORS PART 2

Alexis sends me a screenshot from the producers of the talk show, their list of softball questions tailored for daytime television. She knows what she's doing when choosing which outlets to work with. No hard-hitting journalism, it's too much work. I'm in no mood to field questions about underage sex workers or virginity auctions. It's a long walk from our cars to the studio, maybe a mile, but I've made the trek before. This is my second appearance on the show. I hope this goes better than the last.

"I'm actually a repeat guest," I tell our escort, who doesn't seem to care.

Alexis shakes her head, knowing I'm half joking but also serious. The sugar baby we cast for the show, Harmony, is waiting inside the dressing room in a satin yellow duster. She's lovely, soft spoken with long curly hair tied half up. Harmony is a single mom who met a man on Seeking that helps her take care of her child, a golden case study.

"Hi, Harmony, how are you?" Alexis asks, but something is off. Harmony's energy is cold, quiet.

"I'm okay, really nervous," she says, her hand shaking as she strokes her curls.

"You're going to do great," I tell her. "I'll do most of the talking."

Her presence is enough to sell our message. At least she showed up, and that's half the battle. She probably thought she'd get sued if she didn't, but I try not to think about that. After dropping our bags in the dressing room, we're hustled into the green room, a holding tank with monitors playing the return feed of the show.

"Can I talk to you for a minute?" Harmony asks Alexis, tapping her on the shoulder like a kid who needs the teacher's attention.

"Of course."

Alexis moves to the far corner of the room away from any staffers who might be lingering in the hall. I can't make out exactly what they're saying, but I get the gist. Harmony is getting cold feet just seconds before we're supposed to go on the air. I start milling over excuses. Family emergency, her daughter called, she got her period …

Just then, the producer pops her head in the doorway and gives us the cue. "Walking in thirty, are we ready?"

"We're ready!" I say.

Harmony hangs her head then nods slightly, which can only mean they've reached an agreement. The three of us follow the producer down cement halls past structures that appear to be constructed from popsicle sticks and gaff tape. When we turn the corner onto the set, we feel the Hollywood Magic. We take our seats in front of the audience.

"Please welcome the podcast hosts of *Let's Talk Sugar*," the main host announces. "We're also joined by Harmony, a sugar baby herself." He's a handsome doctor from *The Bachelor* turned talk show personality. Harmony cracks a shy smile.

"How old is the average sugar baby?" the female host asks.

"Well, you have to be eighteen to join," I clarify. "But there are some older, or more mature, sugar babies on there."

"Do you screen these men to find out if they're married?" This time the lady host takes a more condescending tone.

"We do allow married men on our site, and we encourage them to be honest about that," I say.

To my shock the audience boos me. *Fucking boos? What is this, Jerry fucking Springer?* I try not to let the heckles throw me off my game. Alexis laughs at the ridiculousness of it all, but the crowd is not laughing with her.

"Some of them are in open relationships, I mean, it's 2018 people, come on!" I retort.

"I want to hear from Harmony," the lady host says, upending the sneers. "What is this relationship like for you?"

"I'm not looking for a regular relationship. I want someone that's financially stable," Harmony says. "I have a son to take care of, and I can't do it on my own. I'm a single mom," she continues. "I'm in the fashion industry and was able to get pointers and advice from my sugar daddy, so it's a mentorship too."

Afterwards, Alexis and I wait for our Uber behind the studio. "That went well," I snap a selfie. "Harmony is great, but I feel bad for her. What happened in the green room?"

"I doubled her pay so she wouldn't walk out on us," Alexis says, and my heart sinks.

Another poor sugar baby burned by this website and its insidious arms. On the ride, I remember when I joined Seeking, thinking back to my first date when I was played like a fiddle and left addled and embarrassed. I need to get out, but the train is already in motion. LA for the week, then NYC, London, Atlanta. It's easy to forget and make excuses when I'm on the move. Just one more month and I'm out. That's what I've told myself at the end of every month for six of them. This time, I mean it.

Chapter 66

Who is Reflex Media?

I'm four minutes late because I want to sit in the back. The CEO started calling company-wide meetings after Jackie left, his attempt to get everyone on the same page. I see now she was shielding us, designing a company structure where no single person holds too much information or responsibility. I remember about a year into my tenure here they fired a guy whose title was IT and Data. He handled it all. I asked why he was let go since everyone seemed to like him. I was told, "He knew too much." I didn't get it then, but I do now.

I've collected and added pieces to the jigsaw puzzle that is Seeking over the past five years. Details and facts, grievances and anecdotes. They all sit in piles, scattered on the coffee table in my mind. Only recently I've begun to allow myself to put the fragments together, connecting the links and recognizing the patterns. At twenty-six, I can't feign ignorance anymore. Now I'm the one who knows too much.

So, another monthly meeting convenes in the dated auditorium under the skylight that hasn't been dusted in a decade, a room full of strangers. The theme is team presentations, something Jackie would never have done. A member from each team has prepared a PowerPoint detailing what they do at this organization. Silly CEO, Jackie siloed the departments on purpose.

At this point, I'm the employee with the longest tenure at the company. I might be the only one still here who understands our divided accountability. Each person in this room is complicit in contributing to tactics and nudges that prey on would-be sugar babies and guide them to lives of inadvertent sex work. As each team gets in front of the class and gives their spiels, it's like I'm listening with new ears, ones that aren't lying to me anymore, not rationalizing the obvious.

I was inducted and instructed in Seeking's public relations department. Their efforts have convinced many naïve and trusting souls to join Seeking. The pitches are bullshit, the case studies are paid for, and participants trained to lie on this company's behalf. Media outlets turn a blind eye to the obvious holes in our story in favor of clickbait and sweeps. As news cycles repeat, more and more unsuspecting young people with sugar baby ambitions are lured to the website. Many are pulled into sex work, like I was. The benefits are nothing to be ignored until the bottom falls out, the consequences paid by sugar babies.

Customer support staff are the front line in redirecting member complaints. Sugar babies and daddies aren't coming to customer support to tell them how great Seeking is, they're coming with problems. Sometimes it's a bug with the website, but mostly it's member complaints, or "reports," as they're called internally. When a sugar baby is victimized, frauded, or raped, customer support fields her report. While they don't kick the offender off the site, they may suspend the sugar daddy's account and give him a slap on the wrist.

He's given a nudge, made to tick a few boxes that promise he'll take his talk of payments for sex off the site. So long as he coughs up the ninety-nine dollars per month, he's welcome to stay, soon returning a little wiser. As for the victims? Customer support tells sugar babies to report illegal activity to local authorities. The only way to find the identity of an abusive member is through a subpoena. After all, what jurisdiction does a website have? Or at least, that's what we tell them.

Billing handles processing of credit cards. Seeking has a problematic status with merchants because of the high rate of discrepancies. *Honey, it wasn't me, I swear!* In rare instances, when a repeat offender is booted from Seeking, his credit card details become blocked from paying for his subscription until he agrees to the Terms and ticks those little boxes pledging honorable behavior on the website. He might call the billing department to express his annoyance, and they simply tell him to be good and reinstate his card.

Product design is where the intricacies of the system materialize. Using data from Google Analytics, cookies, and other means of tracking, the product team creates a website that keeps members logged on for the longest amount of time possible. The more time the average user spends on the site, the higher Seeking's search rankings. It's the company's primary objective as directed by The CEO, to build a place where sugar daddies eagerly pay for access.

They boast many tweaks and features that help contribute to victimization such as the "New Sugar Baby" badge on profiles created within the last month. Fresh meat, if you will. An easy marker for naiveté, someone who likely hasn't been touched by bad actors yet. She'll learn soon enough. It's the fault of the product team that the website promotes anonymity at every corner, like the note next to the username field that says, "Don't use your real name" and other equivocal mechanisms.

Development – run by The CEO's sister in Asia – is where the code monkeys hang. This arrangement and these procedures result in slow workflows but make sense from a legal standpoint. Spreading the blame across continents means the company is difficult to prosecute, since it's made up of four separate entities that I know of. In addition to development in Asia, The CEO recently moved moderation to the Philippines, a country with notoriously lax execution of laws regarding child labor and child pornography.

Then there's digital marketing, the masterminds behind campaigns that specifically target impoverished and underprivileged women, encouraging them to become sugar babies. People searching the internet for waitress jobs, looking to make fast cash, or trying to get help paying for tuition are hit with ads. They also advertise to men looking for escorts or porn stars, exploiting desperation on either side of the spectrum.

Data is where the secrets hide in plain sight. No one can possibly know how bad things really are, unless they run the data. Thanks to the EU's General Data Protection Regulation, the company can only keep information stored for seven years, which happens to coincide with the statute of limitations for sexual assault in most states. Anonymity plus no evidence equals no crime. You don't have to be a lawyer to figure that out.

And then there's my team. With *Let's Talk Sugar* and social media, sex work is normalized, spawning a spurious sisterhood. It might be the worst of all, parading around like I'm helping. Recently I realized an unfortunate truth. Glorifying the sugar lifestyle is a way to train a force of women who allow bad behavior from men and spread their legs without pushback for a few hundred bucks.

I'm the first one to leave the room, pushing the metal double doors like a linebacker. Outside I take a breath, get some air, recalibrate my emotions. Why am I allowing myself to stay stuck? For what? The check isn't worth me going insane. I take a deep breath, go back to my desk and pull up a job search.

CHAPTER 67

FREEDOM LIGHT

I run into Gabi in the hallway, a coworker I went to Cabo with several years ago for a video shoot. We used to be close but hardly talk anymore. She recently transitioned out of PR and has been taking on some of The CEO's half-baked projects. He's constantly wanting to launch some new startup. First, it was an app for burner phone numbers, then a mobile haircut service, an at-home STI test kit, too many to count.

"Hey girl, what have you been up to?" I ask.

"I'm working on Freedom Light," she says with a subtle grimace.

"What's *Freedom Light*? I've never heard of it."

"It's the charity The CEO wants to start. I'm working on the application," she says.

"What charity? For what?" I'm confused and a little concerned. What business does The CEO have starting a charity? What sort of tax-exempt scheme is he up to now?

"It's for victims … of sex trafficking," she says after a pause and shrugs.

"Sex trafficking?!" I nearly choke. "Is he fucking *serious*?"

Gabi looks behind her, checking the hall for ear hustlers. "I know." She tilts her chin down and shuffles papers she's holding, slowly shaking her head. "I know."

We look at each other like two people who are just doing their jobs, out of control of it all. She goes back to her office, me to mine, dismissing the air of shameless discordance around this new scene in our several-act play. I can see the drama unfolding in court: The CEO pleads his case to the honorable Judge Whatever. *I would never support sex traffickers! SEE! I have a charity that's ANTI-SEX TRAFFICKING!* The only question left: will they buy it? The jury is out. And I would like to be out too, permanently out.

Chapter 68

Good Morning Britain

Las Vegas air slaps me like a furnace as I get out of the car, wrestling with my suitcase since my Uber driver isn't particularly abled. It's nice to get out of town, I'm just not happy to be going on national television once again with this sugar baby circus. I feel like the bigger the interviews get, the more I'm hurting my chances of working elsewhere. Who wants to hire a hooker? The quiet acquiescence is making my acne flare up; I itch the blemish forming at my hairline.

I meet Alexis in the United lounge before our flight, business class as usual. We enjoy the spoils of this job, the cush salaries and bottomless expense accounts. The only saving grace of this fucked up situation. Alexis has The CEO wrapped around her finger, and by default, I do too. She secured a placement on *Good Morning Britain*. We're hosting a coaching event in London, and then appearing on their talk show for an interview, the biggest one I've done by my account.

"Do you think they'll ask us about the virginity auction?" I ask Alexis, sipping my latte and eyeing her finger sandwiches from the buffet spread.

"I'm sure they will. It was a huge story, and they didn't ask The CEO about it when he was on the show last year."

"Oh, that's right. I forgot he did the show," I say, having blocked the unnerving exchange from my memory. I do that a lot.

But how could I forget? A couple days before the London *Sugar Baby Summit* back in 2017, he went on the air and gave one of his memorable performances. Manic, rife with his signature erratic head movements like an anxious chicken and light bouncing off his oily skin. There was a particularly cringe-worthy moment when he was shaking his fist at the interviewer talking about how sugar babies are *empowered*. The sugar baby opposite him stayed calm and collected, making him seem even more aggressive. It was … quite the interview.

Alexis smiles, "I know, they didn't want him this time. I'm sure *that* ticked him off."

We're the stars now, and I bet he's jealous. Alexis and I have agreed that we will not be going over to his house to hang out either, which probably ticks him off too. It got weird the last time we were there. He offered us loner bikinis for the hot tub. I nearly gagged.

Our call time for the show is 6:00AM. In full glam, armed with our best nonsense, a black cab drops us off in a dark and damp alleyway behind the studio. I take a deep breath of cold, moist air as rain starts to fall, thunder clacking. The producer shepherds us to the set promptly at 6:30AM after we snap a few photos.

The host gets right to it. "Are you basically training women for a form of prostitution?" *So that's how this is gonna go.*

"Well thanks so much for having us, we're very excited to dispel that myth. What we're really teaching about is Seeking.com, a place where people can find someone who is financially stable. I know a lot of the lads at the pub probably aren't," I say in my flattest American accent.

After some banter, she asks the question I've been waiting for. "There was an investigation, and it did crop up that some women, girls, had put themselves on the website saying they were auctioning their virginity."

I can't help but smile at the absurdity, and the audience will see my side. "I think that was blown out of proportion, and it was actually an old profile that was not active anymore," I reply with the finesse of a politician. Done and dusted.

CHAPTER 69

NEGATIVE HARMONY

"I'm planning Sydney for January or February. It will be summer there," Alexis says in the back seat of a Prius driving down Santa Monica Boulevard. "After that, I'm out."

We're headed to a satellite studio for an interview with *The Morning Show* in Australia. Respectively, each of us has been looking for other work. I was forthcoming about my position at Seeking on my resume, and I think it might be hurting me. I thought the skills would shine but maybe the moral aspect is too much of a risk for corporate employers.

"Same, I've seen some cool job postings but haven't heard anything back yet," I say, dabbing some extra gloss on my lips.

Looking at myself in my phone's front-facing camera, I scan my face for imperfections. I hardly recognize her, the black lined eyes, teased hair and injected lips. Our makeup artist made me look like a straight up prostitute. I guess it's fitting, but it's not me. This isn't me anymore, maybe it never was.

Our coaching event follows the interview. In our car on the way there, we find out the reporter dropped out at the last minute, which seems to happen more often these days. They probably have second thoughts on perpetuating the narrative, and rightly so. It's too late to cancel now. Believe me, I wish we could, but once again the train has already left the station.

"How do you make sure he pays you?" one sugar baby asks.

It's a free-for-all without the press here, no need to keep up appearances or monitor what questions are asked. The crowd of about twenty-five lean in to hear my answer. At this point, I'm three glasses deep and so fucking fed up with these sugar babies. Don't they know they're not supposed to say "paid?"

"Sugar babies aren't paid, they're gifted," I say. "If you want to be gifted, become a sugar baby. If you want to be paid, get a job."

Laughing, Alexis covers her mouth. The sugar babies don't find me so funny. We play a prerecorded video on a wall of screens, a concept we came up with to give us a break during events to make our lives easier.

Once it's over, Harmony emerges from the crowd of liquored up sugar babies. We haven't seen her since *The Doctors*, but I've thought about her. How she tried to follow her intuition but sold her soul under pressure. She wants to speak with Alexis in private. The pair drift out of earshot. I can see Harmony's eyes begin to well up, and I move closer in case I need to run interference.

"I don't know what I'm going to do," I overhear Harmony say, a tear streaming down her cheek, bisecting her dewy bronzer. "I should never have done the show."

Alexis slowly nods, dejected. Harmony's sugar daddy broke up with her after he found out about the segment. I throw back another glass of wine before we leave, but I can't get the image of Harmony sniffling out of my mind. It's been a long time since I've had to face one of these stories head on like Allison or Isabelle. Neither of them will talk to me anymore, and I don't blame them. It's feeling like we're all in the same boat, our professional value diminished by fucking clickbait.

I wake up at 4:00AM with my internal organs on fire. I race to the bathroom and vomit until it's nothing but bile and despair. I succumb to alcohol poisoning – despite what I thought was only a few drinks – and spend half the morning worshiping the porcelain bowl.

NEW YORK TIMES – OCT. 15, 2018 – A "SUGAR DATE" GONE SOUR

> Once they were up in the room, they got down to business. Ms. Fowles asked Ron to pay them upfront. Though Ron had clearly wanted to communicate on the telephone to avoid making a digital footprint with text messages, he said he wanted to pay her and her friend via the PayPal app. He told Ms. Fowles he could write off the expense if he paid it digitally.... It wasn't until she got on the subway and looked at PayPal that she saw her payment request had been ignored.

CHAPTER 70

SUGAR'S MOST WANTED

"Who's the reporter on this?" I ask, my nylons slipping as I cross one leg over the other.

Alexis is pressing her phone to her ear with her shoulder, lining up our Australian tour while she lines up her manicure with a file. I sink into the old cushion on the chair in our hotel lobby, a sinking feeling in my heart. Another coaching event, an A&E special this time in Lower Manhattan. Snow falls lightly outside, collecting in dirty piles of gray mush lining the sidewalks. I get a chill down my back despite a radiator blasting my shins like a toaster oven.

"It's Elizabeth Vargas," Alexis says, chiseling her last nail. "We almost have too many sugar babies for this one. They won't leave me alone."

"Oh, right," I turn my head, and her signature scent soothes me.

The conversation we had last week comes to mind. I pull up a Google search to remember the journalist's face. She used to host *America's Most Wanted*. I remember watching it on the square TV in my living room with my little brother and parents before the divorce. Back then, my dad would play piano in the morning, and then we'd go to church to study life's questions through religion.

I didn't find my most valuable lessons through scripture. I learned them through betrayal and trauma, drunk on my back, reading sugar daddy reports, and hearing first-person stories of abuse. Those are my life's lessons. The truth about what motivates people. The truth about what they do under the guise of anonymity, when they are so sure they won't get caught; when they assume their victims are weak and discredited. The truth is disturbing, and the lies of this company have gone on too long. Nearly a year after FOSTA, Alexis and I are surprised that Seeking is still operational and that we're still here. Last week, we found job listings from Reflex Media … for our positions.

Our coaching event starts soon; my event coordinator reserved a chic spot in SoHo. Books line the walls of the bar like a library with flickering candles dotting the shelves. A hidden door leads to our meeting space and rows of classroom style desks where sugar babies are gathering. Our assistants buzz with branded handouts and notebooks. Alexis and I bring our staff to run the events and manage sugar babies now. We are the talent and can't be bothered anymore.

"You're not drinking?" Alexis asks, both of us riffling through our rented designer handbags.

"I haven't had a sip since LA," I say, leaving a few singles on the bar. "It makes me sick, even the smell."

"Then today will to be rough," she says. "This is our last event until Australia." She looks at the time on her Apple watch. "And it's already halfway over!"

She notices the camera crew arriving and ushers them behind the faux wall of books. I find my birth control pill, swirling my diet coke before swallowing the tiny tablet. I hang back at the bar, trying to stay out of sugar baby sights until it's necessary. I can't stomach another sad story, especially not before my interview with Elizabeth. Just when I think I'm in the clear, a pair of girls manage to find me.

"Brook, right?" One asks, stomping over to me in chunky black boots.

I notice the micro-mini skirt she's wearing despite the frosty temperature outside. "Hi, yes," I tilt my head robotically.

"I'm Erica," she smiles, red lipstick on her teeth. "My sugar baby name is Star. I've watched all your videos."

"Me too!" the other one chimes. "We watched them together." They both laugh; one smells like cotton candy.

Before they can ask me anything, my assistant pulls me for my interview, and I'm grateful. These days, I only like to answer pre-approved sugar baby questions, since most of their queries relate to the nature of their misplaced sex work. I trail off and prepare to disassociate for my interview. I visualize myself afterwards, happy it's over. Before I know it, it is.

CHAPTER 71

A SINKING SHIP

I spark up another joint – my third this morning – and blow a cloud of smoke through the screen into the pouring rain outside. I'm numb, and yes, officially unemployed. Eleven employees including Alexis and me were fired. The CEO cleaned house in a massive layoff eliminating a sixth of the company, and all the dissenters by my assessment. He told me I was no longer a good fit, pushed an NDA across the desk with a handsome severance agreement. I didn't ink the page in front of him, not yet. I want to make him sweat.

The amount of the offer seems like pennies compared to the injustices I've suffered, the lies and coverups I've fabricated. All in the name of a man who is part of the problem. What am I supposed to do, go to the police? Tell them it's a front for sex work, sometimes trafficking? The sick part is they know, and some of them even use the site to pay for sex, I've seen it. Politicians, too. Between them and The CEO, I don't stand a chance. They could kill me and make it look like an accident. I'd be risking my safety if I came forward.

And for what? So he can sue me into oblivion? Being a whistleblower just doesn't make sense for me. Plus, this is a sinking ship. After what happened with Backpage, FOSTA, the string of deplorable crimes and proof of underage girls on the site, I'm lucky to get out now. I want to sign it and wash my hands of this place, of The CEO who makes my skin crawl. But I'm hesitant, reluctant even. I feel underestimated.

What if my silence is worth more than money? If I don't sign, he might do something drastic to keep me quiet. I'd be walking around with a target on my back. He might instruct his intermediaries to go for the bullseye. If I do sign, I'm swearing my allegiance, taking money over morality again. It's a practice I'm skilled at. So I do, falling into my patterns once more, forwarding the signed agreement and a little piece of my soul as an email attachment. Shortly after I push send, I get a call from Alexis. We've only texted in the week since the layoff, and it's nice to see her picture on my caller ID.

"You signed it, right?" she asks.

"Yeah, it seems like our best bet," I reply. "Miss you!"

"I know, I'm going to miss our adventures. I'm sure we'll get asked for comment eventually, like when the site gets shut down."

"Or when we get subpoenaed," I laugh, and she does too, even though neither of us are joking or see the humor in the inevitable.

EPILOGUE

Now, nearly six years later, it's 2024 and I'm almost thirty-three years old. What I've learned during these post-Seeking years might be more severe than the revelations during my five-year tenure. When I was let go in 2019 after FOSTA was passed, I assumed the jig was up and the site would be shut down. I was wrong. As of this printing, it still exists. I've heard whispers that The CEO is a billionaire.

Back in April of 2021, news of a scandal broke. A sitting US Congressman and his tax collector buddy allegedly involved in sex trafficking of minors they met on Seeking. I was contacted for comment by both a legacy crime documentary show and the most noteworthy newspaper in New York. I worked with them respectively – flew across the country to interview – and gave them everything I had.

I felt seen. They understood that The CEO and questionable morals of the website are but smoke and mirrors for what's truly happening: an underground agency for preying on vulnerable populations, including minors, at an alarming rate. I believed that a chorus of strong media voices would surely end this dark corner of the internet and the evil it facilitates; even the law was on our side. Confident that the information had reached the right hands and justice would be served, I decided to write my story, not sure anyone would care to read it.

That was over three years ago. You might be wondering why you never saw those news articles or segments and why the website is still around. Great questions, and I've got a few guesses. But first, I want to break this down more bluntly to help you understand and process what my story reveals about what is happening to our world and about, specifically, sex trafficking in America. It involves media manipulation, bribery and lies, and a sophisticated house of cards.

The commodity in the "sugar daddy website" business is aspiring sugar babies. They're young and impressionable, usually broke, and range from gullible to desperate. Hailing from a generation that worships Disney and the hero arch, the toxic Prince Charming fantasy is deeply rooted in our culture. Most believe, or want to believe, in the pot of gold at the end of the rainbow. Securing a sugar daddy tugs at the delusion. What's wrong with an older man giving a younger person – young enough to be their grandchild in some cases – a little spending money?

Insert Seeking. A website where young people can hypothetically make extra cash by befriending old men with deep pockets. The unfair imbalance of power is glaring. This is a website curated toward sugar daddy preferences and indiscretions. In fact, most "sugar daddies" are not even rich. Would-be sugar babies don't know this, and poser daddies certainly aren't going to tell them. Shady grifters can pick up where Seeking's marketing leaves off and have a bevy of wide-eyed young women at their disposal, all for the low price of $99 per month for sugar daddy membership. A steal if you ask them. Under the guise of anonymity, Seeking is rife with fraudsters, traffickers, and men booted from Backpage.

Even if predators have been kicked off, they can easily make a new profile and restart the cycle of abuse. There are men who have been using Seeking for years, some for over a decade. They keep getting older and sugar babies stay the same age. A crop of fresh eighteen-year-olds find Seeking every day. But for many sugar daddies, being eighteen isn't a requirement. A portion of these men like *very* young girls. There are no background checks required, which welcomes sex offenders and criminals to join the site. Worse, the media attention in cases of underage sex trafficking only leads to *more* sign-ups. It's like a neon sign that says, "*Get your underage girls here.*" It's where politicians meet minors, so it must be good.

To offset the disparities – age, power, and wealth – Seeking touts this lifestyle as empowering for sugar babies. Nothing could be further from the truth. The stories I've heard go more like this: a sugar baby signs up for the site and is quickly preyed upon by scammers, then duped in one way or another. Are they being stupid? Maybe. Seeking executives and staff exaggerate success ad nauseam, lending credence to the systemic lies sugar babies willingly believe. I should know, I was one of them. I was targeted and tricked as a new sugar baby on the site.

The best part for fake sugar daddies? The girls aren't pros. It might seem confusing, but sugar babies don't normally see themselves as sex workers, despite a willingness to be paid for sex. Culprits know this and serially exploit it. The shame of being abused or conned is commonly too much to bear. Victims quietly and all alone try to forget. Like I did. Adding insult to injury, most sugar babies on Seeking are Black women, and they are affected by bad actors at a higher rate.

Too often the blame is placed on the sugar babies who were "asking for it" and set themselves up to get hurt. Believe me when I say, if you have been victimized, you are not alone. It's not your fault. Remember, we live in a society where women are taught to be submissive and ridiculed for speaking up. We're scolded for holding men to account, for hurting their feelings. The agenda is to easily control us and get sex without resistance. We've been conditioned to allow it.

So why aren't litigators taking a closer look at this? Why do law enforcement and policy makers turn a blind eye? Why did they bother creating a bill to regulate and eliminate this type of website in the first place and rarely follow-up on enforcement? I wish I had the answers. I would love to issue a reprint with better news, but until we do something together, this is the future we share. A future where egocentric leaders and lawmakers build a world many of them will not live to see. Where those who dare to fight for what's right fear repercussions. Where career politicians enact legislation that codifies *their* power and benefits *them*, not you. You are not in their thoughts or their prayers. The foxes are watching the hen house, and no one seems to care … just the way they like it.

Back when I was eleven years old on my orange iMac G3, I came to understand the possibilities of the online world. I could be anyone. I chose to be sixteen. That same anonymity is used to absolve powerful criminals and to spy on you, collecting your data and feeding it to AI. Websites like Seeking directly target vulnerable, impoverished communities and possess troves of information on potential marks. I can only imagine what big tech wizards are cooking up with their ever-growing silos of personal data. How are they using it to maintain their control over the largest voting bloc in the country?

People willingly share every detail of their lives on social media hoping for more and more likes. You don't have to wonder what people are thinking; they'll tell you. But it works the opposite way, shaping behavior and perceptions of reality. Demented algorithms are deciding your feelings and your fate. Media is fed lies by criminal's PR reps, just like I used to do during my time at Seeking as a master of "spin." Mainstream media collude with corporations and politicians to paint a pretty picture for the right or the left. Both sides catch and kill stories that don't fit their narrative. They get rich advertising corn flakes, drugs to keep you younger and thinner, then have the audacity to tell you not to believe your eyes when you see the truth. The joke is on us.

The powers-that-be think we're stupid, and I don't want to believe they're right, but look around. They think we're too stupid to make decisions, so they make them for us. They think we're too stupid to vote, and we don't, and they win. What I know now is this: if we don't do something collectively and start giving a fuck real soon, this is the future we share. Renters in debt, living paycheck to paycheck, programmed by technology to stay in line, vote with the party, and *be grateful*. And as for the laws your leaders concoct – in fancy chambers, dressed in designer suits paid for by your tax dollars – enforcing those policies isn't part of their charade, and they believe we're too stupid to notice.

But why did I write this memoir slash exposé? I could have married some rich man and crawled into a mansion somewhere, reducing myself to nothing more than his wife. It might have been easier that way. I've been taking the easy way out most of my life. Burying the guilt and looking to the future, not the past. Today I reflect on the present and think, how did our country get to this repugnant point in history?

For young women today, it started with indoctrination. Slutty characters on TV shows and force-feeding birth control down our throats. I don't take it now; it made me unstable. It makes sense why so many women are emotional. I was a basket case with a short fuse for ten years. Why didn't anyone ever tell me it could be the little pill I took every day? Who was I taking that pill for? I was taught to believe I'm empowered, that I can enjoy casual sex like a man. That was a lie. It's not biologically possible. Reflecting on the real reason why, it's clear to me that belief did not help me, and it was not *for* me. It hurt me more than I could ever understand back then. But I have clarity now without hormones and shame clouding my perception.

I was compelled to write the book I wish I'd read when I was young, before I learned about this fucked up website and before sex work changed me. The road to get there was gradual, but where I find myself now is hardened. Untrusting in relationships, comfortable and happy being alone. When I get involved with a partner, sharing my history of sex work is something I must do to feel honest. Will my potential partner still want me, knowing other men have gotten it so easy? Can they handle it? I'm so selective about who I have sex with now. Plus, our government is coming for women's freedom of choice. They want to control what we do with our bodies, forbidding abortions and mandating unproven vaccines. I need to be extra careful. The stakes have never been higher.

Do I think sex work should be legal? I think people should be able to elect representatives they trust to make and enforce laws that protect women's rights and the basic tenants of democracy. I believe individuals should be able to decide what's right for them. I would never recommend sex work or wish it on my worst frenemy. It's not easy money. It's the most haunting and traumatizing money I've ever made, and I worked for Seeking. But that's my opinion, and I'm not forcing it on, or suggesting it, for anyone. One of the most flagrant issues I see is lack of accountability for the operators of websites that promote and support access to vulnerable young women, many of whom still carry Prince Charming in their hearts.

Getting the site shut down isn't my goal, though it would be welcomed. My goal is to tell you the truth, my truth, in hopes it might help you if you are a young woman, the parent of a young woman, a lawmaker, a journalist, or just someone who cares. If you think I owe you an apology for my work at Seeking, I'm sure I do. I'm sorry, and I mean that. It's fucked up. I did that. I wrote that. I said what I said. And I'm just getting started.

* * * * *

A NOTE ABOUT WHERE TO FIND ME...

I won't be in the comments section, I probably disabled them. I didn't write this so you can tell *me* what you think. I want you to tell *the world* what you think. Decide for yourself, then do what you can to correct the injustices around *you*. I created a list of resources and suggestions for victims and allies found at the QR code below.

For those who join me on this journey as a subscriber, (yes, honey, I stay getting that coin) you'll get access to my full catalog of exclusive content and so much more because the secrets between these pages are just the tip of the proverbial iceberg. Let's build a network of forward thinkers and dreamers and work together forever <3

I can't wait to meet you.

www.brookurick.com

Glossary

Allowance – A set amount per month that a sugar baby receives from a sugar daddy. Most sugar babies never get an allowance, though the marketing makes it seem otherwise.

Backpage – Now defunct classifieds style website commonly used for sex workers and sex traffickers. It was shut down after the passing of FOSTA.

Casting/cast – The internal process at Seeking for recruiting sugar babies to participate in media like TV news for a fee.

FOSTA/SESTA – shorthand for Allow States and Victims to Fight Online Sex Trafficking Act, a US law that was passed in 2018 leading to the shutdown of Backpage. Before this law, it was more difficult to prosecute websites contributing to sex trafficking. After this law, Seeking and websites like it could be prosecuted, too. SESTA is another similar bill and the two (FOSTA-SESTA) were combined to reach a common goal. Find more info at congress.gov.

Girlfriend experience (GFE) – Escorting term that refers to a type of experience for the client where the sugar baby or sex worker, whatever they want to call themselves, acts as though she is the client's girlfriend, usually for overnight visits, dinner dates, etc. It involves more emotional labor since they need to pretend they actually like him.

Louboutin/Loubies – Designer shoes with a red sole, known as "red bottoms." This is a status symbol and flex for sugar babies, with owning a pair being the main objective of some.

POT – Shorthand for potential sugar daddy as coined by the online sugar baby community.

Pay-per-meet (PPM) – A type of arrangement in which the sugar daddy pays the sugar baby per meeting rather than a monthly allowance.

Salt daddy – Also known as a predator. Name coined for fake sugar daddies by the online sugar baby community. Can also refer to men who have no intention of giving money to sugar babies but lie and manipulate to get what they want. The website is full of salt daddies to the point that it's the number one complaint of sugar babies.

Sex trafficking – the action or practice of transporting people from one state or area to another for the purpose of sexual exploitation, commonly known as pimping. This is like when one man finds a woman on Seeking and takes her to another man, who then pays for sex from the woman.

SEX WORK – The act of exchanging sexual acts, sex services or performances for money. Can include direct physical contact or indirect sexual stimulation. I prefer the term "sex worker" over "prostitute" because it's less derogatory and has less sexist connotations.

SEEKINGARRANGEMENT (SA)/SEEKING – "The world's largest sugar daddy dating site" was the marketing line. That may be true, but it's also one of the largest places for sex work, sex trafficking and general predatory behavior. During the early years, we called it SA, or SeekingArrangement. During a rebrand in 2017, they dropped "Arrangement" completely, which is when I start referring to it as simply Seeking.

SPLENDA DADDY – A man who wants to be a sugar daddy, but simply isn't rich (or perhaps generous) enough to be a sugar daddy. They're not bad actors, not looking to manipulate women, just not rich.

SUGAR BABY (SB)/BABY/BABIES – Usually this is in reference to a sugar baby member of Seeking, since that's what the account type is called on the website. It also refers to the people behind those accounts who might identify with any gender. Most often they are young women, and about half of all sugar baby accounts are Black women. There are male sugar babies and gay sugar babies, too. I don't get into those in this book, but I plan to with other content on my website. Bonus word: Gaybies are gay sugar babies.

A note on the capitalization of sugar baby and sugar daddy – When I worked at Seeking, we would always capitalize them. It was a way to establish credibility. I don't want to lend any credibility to either, so I chose to keep it lowercase.

SUGAR DADDY (SD)/DADDY/DADDIES – Refers to men with sugar daddy accounts on Seeking. Usually these are men over the age of forty. A majority are married. Many of them use the website as an agency to pay for sex or to manipulate young women in one way or another.

SUGAR BOWL – Name coined by sugar babies online for the game that is being, or trying to become, a sugar baby and the many nuances thereof. Could also be called the sugar world, an all-encompassing term to describe sugar baby reality.

SUGARING – I first heard this term from Allison, the name for actively seeking and dating sugar daddies.

SUGAR LIFE/SUGAR LIFESTYLE – Name for the spoils and desirable lifestyle of a successful sugar baby. There are a small minority of sugar babies living this lifestyle. It is essentially the sugar baby lottery.

Font clarification

Actual texts and emails are displayed with the font below:

Conversations were copy/pasted and in some cases edited for clarity, but the gist remains the same. For full transcripts, visit my website.

Index